A Kitchen Herbal

MAURICE MÉSÉGUÉ is an author and healer who lives in Provence in France. He is the son of a farm worker and much of his knowledge has been handed down in his family from father to son. Long before he became known as an author he was known as a healer, numbering among his patients the Ali Khan, King Farouk and Pope John XXIII. His reputation as a healer is now worldwide.

MADELEINE PETER is cookery editor of *Elle* magazine, and her ideas and methods are known all round the world. She and Maurice Méségué experimented widely to create the recipes in this book. She is the author of the *Elle Cookery Book*.

Other cookery books available in Pan

A KITCHEN HERBAL

Making the most of herbs
for cookery and health

Maurice Mességué

with Madeleine Peter

Translated by Fay Sharman
with drawings by Yvonne Skargon

Pan Books in association with Collins

First published in Great Britain 1982 by William Collins Sons & Co. Ltd
This edition published 1984 by Pan Books Ltd,
Cavaye Place, London SW10 9PG
in association with William Collins Sons & Co. Ltd
Text © Opera Mundi 1981
Drawings © Yvonne Skargon 1982
ISBN 0 330 28091 0
Printed and bound in Great Britain by
Cox & Wyman Ltd, Reading

Contents

Preface

This is a sequel to my book *Health Secrets of Plants and Herbs* (Collins, 1979). Here I tell you about the origins, the methods of cultivation, the preservation and the use of many of these gifts of nature and I have emphasized their qualities in cookery, always beneficial even when used in small amounts.

The current interest in herbs means where once fresh and dried herbs were to be found only in delicatessens or specialist shops, they are now generally available in greengrocers, markets and supermarkets. Today coriander appears alongside parsley, mint, dill and many others, often grown in places where pollution is unheard of and without the aid of pesticides, herbicides, DDT or other chemicals. This is something I care passionately about and I cannot repeat it often enough: no curative plant, whether it is an ingredient of a dish or merely a garnish, should be treated with chemicals.

From ancient times these herbs and plants were the only known seasonings. The *conquistadores* were not simply motivated by the lure of gold: their over-riding goal was spice—coveted as wealth, an object of piracy and extortion, a source of profit certainly, but also essential to the well-being of the people. In the days before refrigeration the purpose of these powerful aromatics was, above all, to mask the smell and flavour of meat that was rotten, tainted or strongly salted. But this was not their only purpose. Long before the Christian era, herbalists were presenting their wares as remedies for fever, poisoning and witchcraft. The Greek doctors drew up a catalogue of herbs and defined their properties; they were also the first to recognize the importance of food hygiene. Through the centuries, gardeners adapted and bred herb varieties for cultivation, often improving their appearance, but without changing their flavour or qualities, and, in this way, herbs were saved from popular oblivion.

You can grow the most common herbs in the tiniest patch of earth, even in a pot on a balcony, so that you always have a fresh supply; and, thanks to modern packaging, vacuum drying and dehydration techniques, others are available throughout the year, in dried form or as seeds.

In writing this book I have had the good fortune to meet Madeleine Peter, the author of the cookery column in the magazine *Elle*. Her talent was already known to me, and I have always appreciated her concern for balanced cooking: each one of her articles is a lesson in eating well and wholesomely. We have created the recipes in this book together, experimenting with combinations that I have suggested of certain dishes with certain herbs—the thirty-odd herbs and spices which I discuss in the first chapters. Each of the following recipes has an introduction before the method is described since I believe it is right to know about a dish before undertaking the recipe.

Our cookery book includes more than twenty essential sauces, which are within the capabilities of all cooks, even of beginners. Then we proceed to soups, hot and cold and sometimes uncooked: among these are an unusual cabbage soup with Roquefort, the sumptuous broad bean soup with preserved goose or duck from the Languedoc and Gascony to be precise (from the Gers which is my homeland), and gazpacho, the salad transformed into a soup from Spain. There are more than thirty starters to solve, seductively, the problem of menus both for every day and for special occasions. Their ingredients and presentation are fresh, for example, those of quiche with snails—a highly seasoned tart from Burgundy—and tabbouleh, a salad of Lebanese origin which you can buy ready-made but which is always better home-made. Vegetables are well and truly back in favour and, whether it is the authentic gratin dauphinois, red cabbage, or ratatouille from Nice, we have clearly explained the preparation and method of cooking the vegetables. Then comes the produce of sea and rivers, with unusual recipes as well as old favourites which have been updated in their execution and presentation. Meat recipes follow and include those for the increasingly popular barbecue. There is a section on poultry, with the famous magrets or steaks of young grown ducks, prepared in the style of their place of origin—Gascony again.

Here are some superb and exciting recipes; and we end with twenty grouped under the title, 'Fancies, sweets and pastries', which will, we hope, prove a revelation—like the peaches with mint, or Tatin, that jewel of a tart in its authentic version. The crowning touch of any meal, from the simplest to the most elegant, is a good, home-made sweet.

This is, then, an original, well-balanced cookery book, based essentially on those dishes to which herbs impart their healthful flavours, without neglecting others which make up a coherent gastronomic collection. It should be read from the first page to the last, like a traveller's tale through the world of recipes. Each recipe will reveal a new aspect of cooking, a short cut, and throw fresh light on that never-ceasing task of past and present, thereby making it a pleasure to create the happiness around you that these dishes and their ingredients will bring.

Maurice Mességué

Culinary Herbs

Basil

The king of herbs, basil has a unique, inimitable flavour. In Mediterranean gardens its leaves are large, but when grown in pots on balconies or windowsills, they are smaller and paler. It is the 'pistou' of that celebrated soup of the Midi, and is also used in many other preparations. Like chervil, it should not be cooked; neither should it be chopped, but cut into strips on a board or with scissors and added to salads and raw vegetables, or hot cooked vegetables and ragoûts.

For soupe au pistou, which has become known just as pistou, you pound a handful of basil leaves to a paste in a mortar, with a clove of garlic, olive oil and sometimes Parmesan. Then mix into the soup when you serve it.

Basil cures migraine, counteracts asthenia, and is supposed to be infallible against gout.

Bayleaves

Our bay tree is the same as the laurel of the ancients, of Apollo and the Caesars, which was used to crown victors. This is the true laurel of the kitchen garden, not to be confused with the common or cherry laurel of the thickets and hedgerows, which is inedible.

The bay is an evergreen shrub with dark green leaves. It is hardy enough to survive frost; it just loses its leaves and then makes new growth. However, it is advisable to plant it in a south-facing position. In northern climes, grown in a trough or pot, it winters well indoors and even looks decorative if you clip it into a round shape.

In cookery, bayleaves are an essential ingredient of bouquets garnis, marinades and pâtés. When fresh, they should be used in moderation as their flavour is fairly strong, even bitter. Half a leaf will suffice where a whole dried leaf is called for. Powdered bayleaves can be bought, and are usually of good quality. They are particularly valuable when you need to marinate food with little or no liquid.

In the summer, make up a bunch of bayleaves and hang them from the stems in a dry, dark and airy place: this will keep the leaves green (although it does not add anything to their flavour, either in strength or refinement). Equipped with a supply of bayleaves, you can use them in various ways. To get rid of smells in the kitchen, burn a few leaves on a baking sheet or in a saucer. Since bay has the added merit of discouraging weevils, put some among your stores of dried vegetables and flour, perhaps when your country home is left empty in the winter but, more importantly, in centrally heated homes in town.

If bayleaves give an exquisite flavour in cooking, they also stimulate the appetite. Taken repeatedly, they lessen the effects of influenza, colds, chronic bronchitis, and even rheumatism. As both preservative and antiseptic, in pharmacy the bay is a source of oil, extracted from its berries, which is used in the treatment of contusions, sprains and rheumatic problems. It is strictly for external application only.

Bouquet garni

One could talk about bouquets garnis, because there are more than one kind, but basically, the bouquet garni is a bunch of aromatic herbs which is added to a dish composed of or creating its own liquid during cooking. It is firmly tied to prevent the herbs disintegrating and spoiling the sauce, and so that the whole bunch can be lifted out when it comes to serving.

You can easily make your own bouquets garnis and, if there are no other directions in the recipe, you should use parsley, complete with the stalks, a few sprigs of thyme and a bayleaf. The bouquet garni can include, as well as the thyme and bayleaf, fennel, rosemary, savory or any other herbs, always clearly specified in a recipe. Any other herb added to the more traditional mixtures will also be specified, for instance, a stick of celery, a branch of tarragon, or a small bunch of chervil. In Provençal cookery, especially in fish dishes, parsley is not always used as a foundation.

Caraway

Caraway is distinguished from cummin by its small curved seeds, with a delicate flavour and hint of aniseed. It is also known as field cummin when it grows wild.

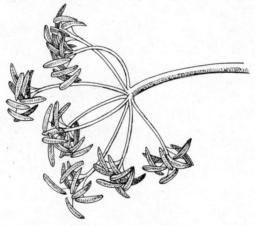

Cultivated on a large scale in the Netherlands, it is used throughout northern Europe and in Russia. You come across it in bread and biscuits, with fish and in stews, in sauerkraut or choucroute, in sausages and other pork products, and in that highly alcoholic liqueur, kummel, much esteemed in Germany and Russia. In the cookery of Germany, Scandinavia and the Balkans, caraway is a familiar flavouring in all the stews and soups, cabbage and potato dishes, and even with baked apples. It is used fairly strongly in marinades for salted or smoked fish, like salmon and haddock, and it flavours the butter sauces served with fish. In France, caraway seeds are little used—you would need to be a well-informed hostess to offer a little bowl of caraway seeds with strong cheeses like Livarot or Munster.

Caraway seeds are rich in mineral salts and proteins, and well-known for their digestive properties. Taken as an infusion, they aid the digestion of heavy, fatty food, and, if you chew the seeds, they help to get rid of the smell of garlic and also encourage the appetite. In short, caraway is good company. Nor do its beneficial effects stop there: it stimulates the brain cells and alleviates heart attacks.

Cardamom

Cardamom appears in the form of small black seeds, enclosed in a capsule like a chick-pea, or of longer shape, depending on its place of origin. In either case, the taste is the same. In the Far East it goes into nearly all the spice mixtures, and is used, for instance, in curries. In Europe, it gets a mention in a few Slavic recipes, and it is one of the flavourings of French gingerbread.

These useful little seeds, hard and black, are an excellent antidote to garlicky breath, and they aren't a nuisance to carry around! In addition, they help to combat wind and, indeed, to aid the digestion.

Chervil

This marvellous herb with a delicate flavour is not as fragile as it seems. Supposedly originating in Siberia, it will survive the frosts in most gardens. Some gardeners sow the seeds amongst the grass after the first cut of the year; when they come to pick it, they spread out the grass and, even under snow, find the chervil as fresh as in springtime.

Chervil should not be cooked or, at least, only very briefly. It is more of a complementary herb, the basis for the mixture known as fines herbes, which is used in omelettes, or on its own as a flavouring for salads or summer an*I* winter soups, added just before serving. Nor should it be chopped, but cut with scissors or broken into flakes with the fingers. Chervil keeps badly, although if you wash it, dry it and refrigerate it in a plastic bag, you can store it for up to a week. It loses its aroma when dried.

When chervil is in season, you can put it to good use by making delicious infusions, which are effective against asthenia and nausea and relieve liver complaints. Above all, the frequent and liberal use of chervil, in salads, soups, and dressings made with cider vinegar, can lend a special touch to the menu.

Chives

Chives come in large and smaller versions, with hollow leaves or stalks. They have a piquant taste, ranging from mild to strong according to size, the largest being very close to an onion. All chives are used in the same way. The Scandinavians make much of them: in Denmark they make a kind of cake of eggs in a frying pan, basically a very thick omelette, cooked slowly over the heat, garnished at the last moment with squares of grilled smoked bacon, and the whole covered with a good layer of chives. These are cut with scissors, never chopped.

A first planting of chives will last for several years in the garden. It is a vigorous plant, dormant in winter but increasing naturally by division of its bulbs. It flowers in the spring, with small, pale pink globes containing seeds which may also sow themselves. However, it is better to cut off the flower heads as soon as they appear, since this makes the plant stronger and enables it to replace more quickly the leaves you have picked. Although they are hardy plants, chives quickly draw up the goodness from the earth—so if you notice the leaves turning yellow too early, sprinkle some compost round the base and water it in. Don't let the plants embark on the winter in a weakened state.

Cinnamon

Cinnamon looks like a small shaving, rolled into a hollow stick. It is the bark taken from young branches of the cinnamon tree, a large specimen related to the bay tree and a native of the Far East, growing from China to India, Madagascar and Ceylon—the source of the finest cinnamon. This has a light-brown colour, with a sweet, slightly peppery flavour and elusive scent. It is a good idea to buy your cinnamon in shavings, not only because these keep better but also because you can be more certain of the quality. Chinese cinnamon also comes in stick form, but is a little larger, a darker brown and with a coarser smell and flavour. It is this kind which is most often sold as powder.

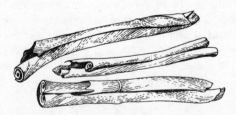

There are dishes, appreciated throughout the world, in which cinnamon plays a major part: in England, the famous Christmas pudding and apple pies, and in central Europe, strudel, either with apples or cream cheese. In France cinnamon is little used and its culinary application is reserved for cakes and pastries, family dishes like rice pudding and the baked or stewed apple of Normandy, chocolate confectionery and various elaborate preparations. However, a discerning palate might recognize a tiny, discreet pinch of cinnamon in certain savoury dishes, such as a civet of hare, wild boar or Barbary duckling or a game salmi of woodcock or mallard. With the influence of North African cooking in Europe, cinnamon has made its appearance in force in the spice mixture known as 'ras-el-hanout'. Like the French quatre-épices, this is a blend of spices, new flavours for some, redolent with memory for others, and enjoyed as much with couscous as with barbecued lamb.

Cinnamon, like many other herbs and spices, is a stimulant, an aid to digestion and an antiseptic for the intestines. Half a teaspoon in a cup of tea will sooth gastric upsets and even diarrhoea. Skiers and influenza sufferers also make good use of it in a glass of hot wine, while some Asian peoples consider cinnamon a panacea for influenza, both preventative and curative, and a stimulant to the circulation.

Coriander

Coriander is the parsley of the East, known under various names such as Chinese chervil and Arab parsley. The fresh leaves, rich in vitamin A, are usually used only in exotic recipes. The whole seeds, on the other hand, have a privileged position. They are used to flavour sausages and other pork products, in all the dishes known as 'à la grecque', in ragoûts, particularly those of pork with haricot beans, in civets, minced meat, and to add strength to curries. You can also fill a peppermill with the seeds and grind a little over stewed fruit such as apples and prunes, as well as spinach, cooked salad greens and cucumber, and braised chicory.

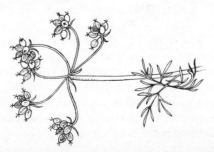

The curative powers of coriander should be stressed. It relieves migraine, ridding the system of the toxins which are often the cause, and eases digestion. A dozen seeds ground into a cup of rosemary tea alleviate period pains.

Cress

There are two varieties of cress—watercress, the kind sold in bunches, and garden cress which is cultivated as a dwarf, curly plant. Watercress is believed to be an excellent green from the health point of view. Very rich in vitamin C, mineral salts and iron, it is recommended for circulatory problems, faintness and anaemia. When it first emerges in spring, it has both purgative and stimulant qualities.

Watercress is a familiar garnish for dishes such as grilled steaks. It is also chopped up with other salad greens and herbs, for use in cold preparations like herb butter, mayonnaise, vinaigrette and cream cheese with herbs, and for fish pâtés. The delightful watercress soup, so refreshing in summer, although rare in winter since the plant is seasonal, should not be forgotten.

If you have a garden, you should cultivate the delicious garden cress, sowing it in the spring and cutting it as it grows. Add it to green salads—lettuce, cos lettuce—and, for picnics, make it into sandwiches with salted butter—fresh and delightful. You will quickly acquire a taste for garden cress, and it will end up in all your herb mixtures, infiltrating the flavour of your hors d'oeuvres!

Cummin

There are several sorts of cummin seed, of varying strength and colour, although it is unusual to be offered a choice of types in the shops. It is in the cookery of the Middle East and North Africa that cummin is commonly employed. The seeds require lengthy cooking and, for this reason, cummin is often sold in small quantities in powdered form, which preserves the flavour well and makes it easier to add the right amount.

Cummin is sometimes confused with caraway. If the seeds do look alike it is worth learning to recognise the difference in scent. Cummin speeds up a sluggish digestion, checking the resulting gaseousness—in fact, it can be called a friend of the digestive tubes.

Dill

The dill of the Scandinavians, 'oukrop' in Russia, is a plant cultivated in northern Europe where it is always eaten fresh, even in winter. In central Europe, as far as the Black Sea, where parsley, chervil and tarragon are uncommon, not to say unknown, you would think it was the one and only culinary herb.

It is easy to confuse fennel with dill, mistaking one for the young shoots of the other. If they are of the same family, their flavour is vastly different. Dill is more delicate, and its thread-like leaves, finer than those of fennel, make an exquisite garnish for fish dishes, salads, and the famous sour cream which is served with cucumbers and even borscht, hot potatoes, smoked fish and the splendid raw salmon with salt.

Like chervil and all soft herbs, dill does not take to being cooked—cooking deprives it of its flavour. It is used as the finishing touch to a dish, in the same way as chopped parsley or fines herbs, but, unlike parsley, it should not be mixed with garlic or olive oil.

Dill is rich in vitamins and mineral salts such as sodium and sulphur. It had an important place in the ancient medical treatises on herbs—the only ones with authority, and it was believed to have the power of stimulating lactation in mothers, and of stopping hiccups and soothing colic in babies. It is said that dill eases digestion and calms a disordered stomach.

Fennel

There are so many varieties of fennel that I shall start with the vegetable, known as Florence fennel. When this plump bulb is eaten raw in salads, it has a discreet aniseed taste, which is totally lost in cooking. Nevertheless, it is valued as a pleasant, delicately-flavoured vegetable, and bridges the fallow vegetable season between winter and spring. Fennel lends itself to many uses and, if you cut off the stems from the base, you can add the little green tuft to salads.

The variety of special interest is the wild fennel which grows in the hills and scrubland of Provence. It has very fine, feathery foliage, which is quickly burnt by the sun and disappears, while the yellow flower cluster or umbel ripens the seeds. The stalks, rapidly stripped, take on the appearance of small wooden sticks, sweetly scented. Nothing is wasted of this typically southern plant: its seeds and stalks crown with glory the meanest gilt-head bream, and give distinction to the celebrated sea bass, known as 'loup' in the south of France and 'bar' on the Atlantic coast. Fennel, caraway, cummin, even aniseed, are all related and vaguely similar, and only the most expert palates can tell the difference between their seeds by chewing them.

Fennel is a stimulant, diuretic, tonic and sedative. Taken as an infusion, the seeds are a cure for worms and help nervous children to sleep. With its soothing qualities, fennel calms coughing fits in whooping cough and works wonders as a gargle for a sore throat. A pinch of the seeds with two or three mint leaves in an infusion relieves wind.

There is another variety of fennel which grows on the European seashore, in Normandy, Brittany and the Mediterranean coast. This is samphire, also an umbelliferous plant, but fatter, with swollen stems and tiny leaves tasting of aniseed and iodine. You will sometimes find it pickled in vinegar as a seasoning, used in certain fish dishes in Brittany or handed round with a stew, poached fish or cold meat.

Garlic

In the Liliaceae family, graced by the lily and lily-of-the-valley, garlic is a poor relation. It came to us amongst the booty of the crusaders, although Virgil had recommended it and the Romans had eaten it. But what does it matter? Today garlic has crossed all the frontiers of cookery.

You may find two kinds of garlic in the shops, subtly different and each with their passionate advocates. One has small, compact heads with elongated cloves coloured light or dark purple; the other is larger and white, with fat cloves.

Spring garlic has a lively but not aggressive flavour. However, from July onwards you must remove the small shoots already forming in the middle of the cloves: split the clove in half lengthwise and take out the green filaments and the sheath enclosing them from each side. This makes the garlic more digestible. In the autumn you should buy a fine rope of garlic and hang it in a cool place, protected from frost, to use throughout the winter. You can usually buy small nets containing a few heads of garlic from greengrocers and supermarkets.

Some people maintain that garlic should not be cut, but crushed with a heavy blow from the flat of a knife blade, or in a garlic press. But for aïoli, the sauce of southern France famous throughout the world, the garlic is pounded to a cream in a mortar before proceeding as for a mayonnaise. For the typically Provençal garnish, too, it is finely chopped with parsley, although for garlic or snail butter it is crushed in a garlic press.

The disadvantage of garlic is that it makes the breath smell. There are all sorts of ways of countering this, most of them inconvenient, such as chewing coffee beans, parsley or chervil, or slowly eating a grated potato with a few spoonfuls of honey. I would recommend mint-flavoured chewing gum! The Orientals, particularly the Chinese, are great lovers of garlic; their solution is to offer cardamom seeds taken out of their pods to each guest to chew at the end of a meal.

But garlic has great advantages: the medical profession recognizes the important properties of garlic. It can be used to combat diabetes and to lower arterial tension. And it has been known for centuries as a powerful antiseptic against intestinal bacteria, as a remedy against worms, and as a stimulant of the endocrine glands (thyroid and suprarenal) and regulator of cholesterol levels.

Allium giganteum, otherwise known as giant garlic, has beautiful pompons, soft blue, mauve or pale pink, at the end of stalks a metre long, sometimes more. The blooms consist of thousands of little flowers which keep on appearing, and they have a pleasant scent and last very well in vases. According to the seed catalogues, they are very easy to grow in any garden.

Ginger

That strange, twisted tuber which is so intriguing in exotic shops is the rhizome of a tropical plant with a very distinctive spicy aroma. It is believed to be such a stimulant that it has the power of an aphrodisiac, and this has endowed it with a certain prestige in the East and elsewhere.

Ginger strengthens oriental spice mixtures, such as curry and 'ras-el-hanout', and many Chinese and Japanese dishes. When you have a fresh piece of ginger, it should be peeled and then grated; but, as the plant is seasonal, it is not always obtainable.

Powdered ginger is milder, and in this form it is used in saltless diets. As a seasoning at table, it does much to enliven food, vegetables as well as soup or meat.

Ginger is very popular in England in ginger ale, ginger beer and ginger wine; you also come across it in traditional sweets like Christmas pudding, in jams and preserves, and fruits in syrup, which should be sampled with caution as the sugar considerably strengthens the spiciness.

Hyssop

Hyssop, like lavender, is one of those bushy garden plants whose leaves you rub as you go past, to breathe in the delicate scent, often without knowing its name or its many uses. In Provençal cookery it is one of the frequently used herbs.

For the purposes of cookery and pharmacy the leaves are picked when the shrub is at its peak, with the pink or bluish flowers just about to open. They are hung up to dry from the base of the stalks in a shady place.

The flavour of hyssop, penetrating but light, places it between rosemary and savory, neither strongly camphorous like the one nor bitter like the other. Like savory it helps in the digestion of meat, those wonderful comforting soups enriched with preserved goose or duck, oily fish, farinaceous food, rich stuffings and sausages and other pork products. A pinch of fresh hyssop leaves, perhaps with chives, parsley or chervil, enhances summer salads and cooked vegetable salads, including potatoes, while you can add it to stewed red fruits, prunes and apples.

On a commercial scale, hyssop has not been neglected and is used in certain liqueurs like Chartreuse and pastis. As an infusion and gargle, it is very effective in the cure of maladies of the respiratory and digestive passages. Hyssop taken in a bath or drink relieves rheumatism; our forbears used to cure lumbago with a poultice of the fresh leaves, chopped and steeped in boiling water.

Juniper

Juniper is a coniferous shrub, unattractive and prickly, which grows in sad clumps in limestone and chalky soil, at the edge of woods and in wasteland. The flowers are fertilised by the bees and the wind, appearing as small yellow cones on the male plants, greeny-blue on the females. The latter ripen into round, black berries, and this is the moment to pick them and dry them in the sun. You can, of course, also buy them.

Although juniper berries have a limited application in cookery, they are indispensable. Their flavour, resinous but mild, adds a light touch to heavy preparations like choucroute, marinades, particularly of game such as venison, wild boar and hare, and pâtés of furred or feathered game. They can be used whole or coarsely crushed; ground in a peppermill, they give a very pleasant tang to grilled meats.

The branches of the juniper bush can be burnt on a barbecue, put on the charcoal at the end of the cooking time, and impart a delicious aroma to meat or fish.

The Scandinavians make digestive infusions with juniper. A teaspoon of the crushed berries in 1 litre (1¾ pints; 4½ cups) of boiling water helps the digestion of starchy foods. Juniper also stimulates the kidneys, acting as a diuretic and reducing inflammation of the bladder, and soothing the whole urinary tract. Rheumatics set great store by it. Gin, both English and Scandinavian, aquavit and various other spirits are based on distilled juniper berries.

Marjoram and oregano

Marjoram is one of the many varieties of oregano, of which there are, reputedly, thirty. To say that they all look alike would not be true, but their flavour and scent are of the same intensity. The garden plant is known as marjoram; it has flowers resembling the buds of a miniature hop plant. The other, wild, type is known as oregano, and carries its tiny flowers in round pincushions at the end of short stalks; it has a more bitter taste according to those who can tell the difference.

Both retain all their flavour when dried. These are the herbs of the pizza and of cooked tomatoes in all their forms, especially the housewife's fresh tomato sauce, and of baked fish, barbecued kebabs and meat stews. The flavour of marjoram may not be appreciated the first time it is encountered, freshly picked, in a salad, but you cannot escape its powers since, even absorbed in minute quantities, it stimulates the digestion.

Marjoram and oregano are often added to soothing drinks for the digestion, such as lime-flower and mint or verbena tea, and they impart a delicate flavour which improves the taste. Taken alone, these herbs have tonic and diuretic qualities; they rouse the internal organs from sluggishness and, at the same time, alleviate pain. They rid the body of many toxins by causing profuse sweating, and help to clear the respiratory passages of mucus and the remains of winter colds and bronchitis.

Mint

Among the innumerable varieties of mint, common mint or spearmint and pennyroyal are the most commonly grown of the edible types used for flavouring. Spearmint has delicate, lacy leaves with pink flowers in small clusters. Pennyroyal has a less obvious scent and groups of small mauve flowers along its stems, reminiscent of wild thyme. Whatever the kind of mint, it brings out the flavour of spring vegetables, peas, salad greens and fines herbes. From China to the Mediterranean it appears in various preparations, hot and cold, as well as in drinks including Champagne cocktails, sangria and mint tea.

Mint preserves its flavour under any circumstances and, fresh or dried, it should be used with moderation in hot dishes. It can quickly dominate, and it is nicer to have a suspicion of its presence than to be overwhelmed by it. Mint is used in the jelly or sauce which goes with English mutton and certain stews, and is very appealing when used in the 'tabbouleh' of the Middle East or the meat balls and barbecued lamb of North Africa. Minestrone or pistou, so strongly flavoured with basil, are also given a discreet touch of mint.

If you ask for an infusion in a French restaurant, the classic recipe is lime-flowers and mint. All types of mint counteract general fatigue, even leading to insomnia, which is the reason for the calming lime-flowers. Mint is also valued for its digestive and stimulating properties. However, it has another quality, little known outside Brittany and India: two or three fresh leaves, rubbed and added to fresh milk, prevent it curdling.

Nutmeg and mace

The nutmeg is a beautiful evergreen tree native to the tropics, the Far East and the West Indies. It is diœcious, that is it has male and female plants, and the flowers of the female are pollinated by insects and the wind. The fruit, which looks like an apricot, opens when ripe in the same way as that of our walnut trees, and releases a stone or nut. This is covered with an aromatic, lacy coating which is stripped off and dried. When reduced to a powder it becomes mace.

The stone is also dried, then cracked open when the kernel inside has become loose. The kernel is the nutmeg we are familiar with, dark brown in appearance and often whitened with lime as a protection against worms, and which ensures its perfect preservation. It is sold whole and grated for use. As its scent quickly diminishes when exposed to the air, it is advisable to keep it in hermetically sealed glass jars or tins.

Nutmeg and mace have the same flavour, although mace is stronger and spicier. Mace is an ingredient of the quatre-épices of stuffings and sausages. Nutmeg is more familiar, in puréed root vegetables, spinach, cheese dishes, stews and in spiced stuffings and pâtés. In winter, it is a seasoning for mulled wine, drinking chocolate and hot milk. In fact, it is enjoyed as much with sweets as with savouries, particularly in Italy, England and Scandinavia. Nutmeg also prevents that drowsiness after the midday meal which so often leads to thoughts of a nap. It can only aid digestion, it scents the breath pleasantly, and it regularizes the circulation, to the extent of improving irregular periods.

Parsley

Known for thousands of years, parsley grows in all the temperate countries. It comes in two forms—the dark-green, plain-leaved parsley, and the paler, milder, curled parsley. The latter is chosen as a decorative garnish for dishes, although cooks consider the former superior.

The virtues of parsley are many. It is rich in vitamins A, B and C, iron and calcium, and is supposed to help children grow. Its antiseptic properties help to combat infections, anaemia, rheumatism and even fibrositis. As a decongestant, it clears the complexion, eases digestion, regulates the functioning of the intestines and, similarly, the liver, and prevents the formation of gall-stones. Used sytematically, parsley leads to both good eating and internal hygiene.

In cookery, parsley is the indispensable and principal element of the excellent bouquet garni, and it is found in almost all preparations involving liquid, such as stews, braises and stockpots. Chopped up on its own or with other herbs, it is a delicious and healthful garnish, while fried it makes a dainty accompaniment to grilled or fried seafood and meat. Chewing the leaves is an antidote to garlicky breath.

To keep parsley for a short time, no more than three weeks, wash and drain it, put it in a plastic bag, seal firmly and store in the fridge. If you want a supply for the winter, prepare the parsley so that it is clean and dry, wrap it in sheets of foil, making small parcels or individual portions, seal hermetically and place in the freezer. There's no point thawing it before use; just unwrap the frozen parsley, crush it between your fingers and it will break into small bits. Don't keep a sad bunch of parsley in a glass of water on the windowsill: it will lose its taste and health-giving properties; it will go bad and be tainted by the impurities in the town air.

Rosemary

This small shrub, which has a place in almost every garden, has one of the most powerful flavours to be found among the culinary herbs. Fresh, dried or powdered, it should be used with great moderation, for its camphorous aroma can very quickly dominate and even destroy the tastes which it is supposed to bring out.

Rosemary occupies a privileged position in Italian cookery: fish, veal, vegetables, pizzas, salads are all discreetly imbued with its flavour and enhanced by it. But its influence is not confined to the Mediterranean countries, and, throughout Europe, from east to west and north to south, it appears in meat and game dishes, sausages and pork products. Yet, like thyme and bayleaf, rosemary is very much at home in sunny, southern preparations using saffron and garlic, in olive oil, with smoked fish and anchovies, with green or black olives and vegetables à la grecque.

It is usually one of the dried herbs stocked by the housewife in her store cupboard, and is not used just for cooking. A small bunch of the larger branches smouldering in the fireplace will scent the whole house. The curative virtues of rosemary are many: it improves circulation, stimulates liver function and gives muscular tone. Recommended for chronic bronchitis and asthma, it is often used as a fumigation. It also brings relief to sufferers of rheumatism and gout.

Sage

In origin, sage is a wild herb from the northern shores of the Mediterranean. It has now been cultivated for so long that nurserymen have had plenty of time to develop several varieties, all sweet-smelling, but with different flavours and each distinguished by the shape and colour of its leaves.

It is a medicinal sage, an evergreen with small, grey, velvety leaves, that is used in cookery. With a slightly camphorous scent, it is one of those rare herbs to be employed on its own, and its flavour is enough to stamp a dish with its seal—goose or pork with sage, stuffed chicken, chick-peas, broad beans or haricot beans. The leaves are stripped off for preservation, and kept in tightly-sealed glass jars in a dark place.

It is always used alone, and not as part of a herb mixture. It does not stand boiling or heating on a grill or in a frying pan, which destroys its delicate flavour, leaving only the camphor. Sage should be added to soups, like the Italian minestrone and the French pistou, only at the point of serving. Its contribution is less exclusive in cold preparations, especially marinades where its presence is countered by the sweetness of the carrots and onions and the flavour of other herbs and spices. It is essential, however, especially with game and water fowl.

Sage has an important role in Italian cuisine, which is based on traditions stretching back to antiquity. It always appears in dishes based on fairly crude olive oil or animal fats, and, in fact, its presence is particularly designed to assist the digestion of fatty and starchy foods. Sage has long been one of the principal medicinal plants; indeed, its name comes from the Latin 'salvia'—that which saves. Its antispasmodic action controls nervous tremors, pains, nausea and asthma. It is effective against tiredness caused by the menopause and restores vitality to the body.

Savory

We know of two varieties of savory: the garden plant, annual savory, and the mountain savory which grows wild on the barren mountain slopes and arid, open scrubland around the Mediterranean.

Both kinds of savory have a slightly peppery flavour and echoes of thyme, rosemary and mint, with a delicacy which demands that they be used sparingly. Too much savory can lead to bitterness. A pinch of the leaves or a small sprig is enough to add to the other herbs in a stuffing, pâté or starchy soup and, indeed, savory is rarely used on its own. It is also highly esteemed, like fennel, for the scent it gives to charcoal-grilled fish or lamb, placed on the embers at the end of the cooking time. In the same way as thyme, savory is useful when you are frying meat in an enclosed space: heat it in the fat in the frying pan and, as well as flavouring the meat, it will give off a pleasant perfume which masks the cooking smells.

The annual garden savory is more hardy than the mountain variety. It should be sown by scattering lightly on the surface of the soil, previously enriched with compost, in an open situation and kept plentifully watered. It increases naturally, and haphazardly, by self-sowing, and, as in the case of many similar plants, it is best to allow this.

To preserve savory, pick it in bunches or uproot the whole plant just before it flowers, and hang from the base in a shady place or dry atmosphere, not in the sun. Don't hesitate to make a good supply, because, taken as an infusion, savory has many uses. In the Middle Ages it was recommended against gout, meaning, in the light of present knowledge, that it takes care of digestive disorders which have been caused by a build-up of toxins and can lead to rheumatism, as well as other maladies, ranging from stomach cramps to asthmatic attacks and smoker's cough.

Star anise

It is neither a small plant nor a shrub which produces star anise, the star-shaped fruit with a shiny seed, strongly aniseed-flavoured, in each of its points. It is a tree native to the Far East, with lustrous evergreen foliage like a magnolia, known variously as Chinese or Indian anise. The crushed seeds are used in curries and many other local mixtures, like the garam-masala of India, a spicy blend of thirteen ingredients.

Star anise is not confined to the pharmacy, but goes equally well in infusions, marinades or ragoûts; always used sparingly—discreetly employed, it is delicious, but if overdone, it is unbearable. The pretty stars keep very well in firmly sealed jars or metal containers and, because of their effectiveness in dealing with an upset stomach, swollen abdomen or difficult digestion, it is always worth having a small stock to hand.

Star anise is very popular from Europe to the East. The aniseed-flavoured bread of Sweden is made with it; spread with butter, this bread is much appreciated by tourists grappling with hearty portions of salted and smoked fish and meat. In Germany it goes into cakes and pastries, while in France, it appears most commonly in aniseed-flavoured drinks and liqueurs, and also in toothpaste. In China, star anise is a flavouring in some teas.

Tarragon

Tarragon comes from the plains of Siberia and the western regions of North America, and was introduced into Europe by the crusaders. It was the 'tharchoûm' of Arabia, whence the derivation of the name—after various corruptions like 'dragon'. However hardy and resistant it might have been in its native land, elsewhere it usually demands some care. It needs a rich soil and good position to flourish. In the winter it loses its leaves, and the small, shy flowers never have time to release their seeds; instead, it increases itself naturally by division.

This fussy little plant has established itself through its inimitable flavour: it is often dubbed the aristocrat of fines herbes and is essential to that mixture. Tarragon makes its contribution without detracting from the total effect, and thus lends distinction to many culinary preparations in its own right. Vinegar, gherkins and mustard are all enhanced by it; spring chicken, cockerel and pigeon are enriched by it, as well as rabbit and oily fish, for instance eel prepared 'au vert'. Tarragon is always used in cold herb sauces. It is evident in béarnaise sauce, lobster and other shellfish with cream, or herb butter for grilled meats; and it improves and flavours jellies.

At the height of its season, the presence of tarragon is as necessary as parsley or chervil. And in winter? When dried or dehydrated, it has no taste—occasionally, you can find it in specialist shops but, generally speaking, it is not available from December to the end of February.

I should include here a method of preserving tarragon which is often recommended, although I have not tried it myself. Addicts of this gem of a plant advise that, at the beginning of summer when the bush is at its peak, covered with fine leaves and beginning to flower, you should pick the stalks and tie them into bunches. Wash and drain them, plunge into plenty of boiling water for one minute, then refresh immediately in cold water. Dry them carefully without crushing. Take a glass preserving jar of 1 litre (1¾ pints; 4½ cups) capacity, fill it with water which has been boiled and allowed to cool, and add 60 g (2 oz) of salt per litre. Put in the tarragon with the tips of the stalks downwards, seal the jar and keep in a dark place.

If you have a freezer, you can pick the tarragon at the same time of year, strip off the leaves, wash them and dry thoroughly. Wrap them in foil, making several small parcels and, if tarragon behaves like parsley, it will retain all its flavour.

You can make an infusion with tarragon, putting a sprig in each cup. This is very welcome after an excellent, but rather too rich meal. It relieves an overworked stomach, without slowing digestion, and soothes a grumbling intestine.

Thyme

There are many varieties of thyme in existence, all with similar flavours and uses. Garden thyme is the one that is available throughout the year; it is one of the ingredients of the bouquet garni and develops all its pungency in cooking and marination.

In the spring, you will find plants which can be grown in pots, but they should really be planted in the garden, where they will increase naturally by seeds, layering or division. In cold areas they need protection in winter with dry leaves or straw, or by banking up the earth around their roots. To ensure a supply until the next season, thyme is dried by hanging it from the roots or spreading it out in a dark place. You can also buy dried thyme leaves, which keep very well in sealed glass jars, shaded from the light—a good alternative if you live in town, where there is rarely room to make your own.

All the aromatic herbs used in Europe originate in the south and, particularly, around the northern shores of the Mediterranean. There, many different sorts of thyme, all with fairly powerful scents, are in common usage. They are known under various names—the 'serpolet' or wild thyme of the Alpilles was beloved of Alphonse Daudet. They grow wild in barren, rocky soil exposed to the sun, and are picked in May when they are in flower. In some villages, the harvest is celebrated with a thyme festival.

Wild or cultivated thyme is one of the essential herbs of Mediterranean cookery. Allied with garlic and olive oil, it appears with fish, and also with goat's milk cheeses, which are at the same time preserved in the mixture and enriched with its new flavours.

There is another variety of thyme which was traditionally used as a border in the vegetable plot and which has now gained ground in European kitchens. This is the lemon thyme of the gardeners, a native of North America with rounded leaves and pretty red flowers. It will not stand cooking, which removes its very individual lemony flavour, but it gives endless pleasure in salads and in vinaigrettes served with seafood.

Thyme is a healthful plant. It stimulates the circulation and alleviates singing in the ears. As a diuretic and antiseptic it is prescribed for urine retention, which often accompanies infections.

Spices

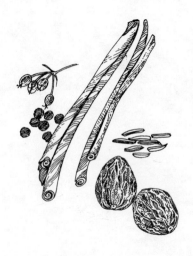

Cloves

The clove tree, a beautiful tree with clusters of pink, bell-shaped flowers, was long the principal resource of Zanzibar. Cloves are the flower-buds, boiled, dried and smoked. In the sixteenth century, the cultivation of cloves resulted in conflicts and stratagems on an epic scale, with every explorer-discoverer of those fabulous lands, the Spice Islands, trying to establish production for their own profit. It was in the reign of Louis XV that Governor Poivre stole the few flourishing plants from under the nose of the Dutch who had the monopoly in the Indian Ocean, and introduced them to all the tropical countries of the globe, where they prosper still.

This excellence spice has a very strong, individual scent. It is used, in moderation, in stockpots and stews, and stuck into onions so that they can be easily located and removed once they have served their purpose. They are found in almost all spice blends, in sausages and pork products, in syrups and in fruit liqueurs.

Cloves appear in perfumery and even in pharmacy. They are an ingredient of toothpaste, although the time has passed when dentists would dip a cotton plug in oil of cloves to sterilize tooth cavities. Nevertheless, cloves remain one of the best natural remedies for sore throats and coughs. They are mixed with an essence made by boiling elder-flowers and berries, and sweetened with honey, adding at least 10 cloves per litre (1¾ pints: 4½ cups). An orange stuck with cloves is a decoration for the Christmas tree and a perfumed pomander for the cupboard. The scent lasts for a long time and, although the orange shrivels and turns brown, it is still ornamental and continues to smell pleasant from one Christmas to the next.

Curry powder

In the first place, we should remember that curry powder, called 'masala' by the Hindus, is a mixture of spices, generally including coriander, cardamom, nutmeg, ginger, cummin, pepper, cloves, cayenne pepper, and sometimes augmented by turmeric, which makes it a deeper yellow. Turmeric, the saffron of India, is a rhizome like ginger, with a very spicy flavour, and is almost never used on its own in European cookery.

Madras curry powder can be found in the shops. It has a beautiful yellow colour and makes a fine, smooth sauce with a taste which is very acceptable to informed palates. A second curry powder which has its followers is Pondicherry, with a different flavour and a darker, more ochre colour. This is the favourite of people who learnt to appreciate it in Indochina and the Island of Réunion. These two are the best-known, but there are plenty of other curry powders.

Whatever the type, you should buy your curry powder in shops with a good turnover and, if possible, in tins rather than glass jars; the light spoils the spices and, besides, you will use it by the tablespoonful and jars do not usually contain enough to last any length of time. Once you have opened the tin it is important to reseal it tightly, as the powder easily goes stale in contact with the air.

In India and Malaysia and all the oriental countries where food is strongly spiced, curry powder is made up at home, using a mortar, and is usually more fiery than the ready-prepared type for export. You can restore hotness with a pinch of cayenne and a few coriander seeds although, in the opinion of the experts, the bought curry powder is by far the best.

Its use in recipes is always clearly specified, and it has become increasingly common in sauces with eggs or fish, and in stews of pork, veal or chicken, served with rice. It is then that chutney, a spicy jam of exotic fruit like mangoes, comes into its own; you can also offer dishes of grated coconut, yoghourt with herbs, almonds, peanuts, sliced bananas, raisins and various other delicacies, some of them designed to heighten the spiciness of the dish, others to counteract its heat.

None of the curry powder mixtures is lacking in beneficial or healthful effects. They don't appeal just to the taste buds: like all oriental spices, used daily they are necessary stimulants in a sultry climate, as well as internal germ-killers—remedies of vegetable origin which can be found in other forms in pharmacy.

Pepper

Since ancient times pepper has been the most common spice in Europe and was once even used as money. It was in search of pepper and the Spice Islands that the Portuguese fleets rounded the Cape of Good Hope in the fifteenth century. Originally from the equatorial forests of Asia, where it grew as a creeper, pepper is now cultivated as a shrub in all tropical countries.

Until very recently, the cook scarcely knew of any other type of peppercorn than white and black. The latter, with wrinkled skins, are the berries picked before they reach maturity and dried in the sun, while the former are in fact the ripened kernel of the berries, with the outer husk removed by soaking and scraping before they are dried. Each has its uses. Black pepper has a stronger flavour, and the softer white pepper is chosen for pale sauces like beurre blanc and hollandaise and for white stews. They should be bought as peppercorns and, as they keep very well, you can get in a good supply for refilling your peppermills. Once ground, their fleeting aroma is quickly spoilt, and the multitude of peppermills on the market testifies to the importance of using only freshly ground pepper.

Mignonette pepper is a ready-made mixture of white and black peppercorns, crushed not ground, and used especially with grilled meats, peppered steak and in certain stuffings.

In the last few years, green pepper has made its appearance among our spices. It is the same berry, picked when green and unripe and preserved, either in tins after sterilization or dehydration, or frozen when fresh and vacuum-packed in bags. It is also found in oil or vinegar, and in a highly esteemed mustard. Unlike other types, green pepper is crushed with a pestle or rolling pin before use.

Cayenne pepper is not a type of pepper but a pimento from the Island of Réunion or the West Indies. It may be sold in the form of small dried pimentos which you crush between your fingers, but it is more practical to buy it as a powder. Use it very sparingly: the point of a knife or the tiniest pinch is enough to pep up the flavour of any preparation, and this means that it never appears on the table as a seasoning. It gives a hot spiciness to oriental cooking.

All the types of pepper, taken in moderate doses, encourage the gastric juices and secretions of the liver, but, beware, since excessive amounts spoil the taste of the food and irritate the whole digestive system.

Pimentos and peppers

Pimentos and peppers are two different plants, although both belong to the Solanaceae family. The first is a vigorous, fruit-bearing shrub, and the second an annual, leguminous plant.

The pimento, with numerous cultivated varieties throughout the tropics, is familiar in the form of small, strong, dried fruits, known, incorrectly when powdered, as cayenne pepper. One type, sold as chilli powder, is a blend of herbs and spices including cummin, garlic and marjoram. This is easier to use than the fresh pimento or its undiluted powder, which can have the effect of dynamite! Tabasco, based on various pimentos and herbs, is a sauce which comes in glass bottles. This, too, has the advantage that it can be measured out in drops and is handy for adding a zing to salads, drinks and sauces.

The pimento acts as a tonic, internal germ-killer and digestive, and is rich in vitamin C. In its native country it is a remedy against fevers, chills and parasitical infections of the intestines.

The sweet pepper is a beautiful green vegetable, turning red when ripe and also becoming more delicate in flavour. It is available in the shops for almost the entire year. As both a vegetable and seasoning, it is eaten raw or cooked, although some people find it indigestible in its raw state. It is more palatable and less sharp if peeled. Sweet peppers are dried and powdered to make paprika, much employed in the cookery of the eastern Mediterranean, North Africa and Spain, where it gives colour and flavour. A stronger, spicier paprika is used in the Balkans.

Saffron

Saffron, both spice and colouring, is the most expensive of all aromatic plants and is rarely used in its natural state, except in

Mediterranean and Far Eastern cookery. It is available in stigmas, which are beautiful, orangey-red threads, or powder; personally, I prefer the former, as the price of powdered saffron leads me to suspect its purity.

Where does saffron come from? It is a beautiful crocus, with blue or pink flowers and long, thin leaves—a bulb cultivated in mild climates, in rich, well-drained soil and in a sheltered position. When the flower is completely opened, the three long stigmas, which hang down when they are ready, are plucked out. All this work is done by hand and, when you realise that it takes about two hundred thousand flowers to make one kilo (2 lb) of saffron, you won't be surprised at the price. But you need very little: only a pinch is required to achieve the desired taste and colour. Good saffron comes in small, bright-red filaments, brittle and very scented; it is like musty hay when old.

To use saffron wisely, dry it just before required on a sheet of foil, either in a gentle oven or on the lid of the saucepan in which the prepared dish is being kept hot; then break it in your fingers, first making sure that they are quite dry, and add. For a very liquid preparation like rice or fish soup, just put in the threads as they are. Recipes where saffron is called for are usually explicit on the subject, and you should keep to the amounts indicated. The flavour and colour do not develop immediately, and too large an amount can result in an overwhelming bitterness and unpleasant colour.

Saffron acts as a powerful internal germ-killer. Over the centuries, before the spread of refrigeration, it probably prevented a great deal of food-poisoning in those warm climates where it is still much employed. Ten years ago I used to buy saffron from the chemist, but now you can find it in many food shops.

Sauces

Aïoli

This is the celebrated garlic mayonnaise of the south of France, and is based on garlic pounded to a purée in a mortar. But be careful: it's not just any garlic, but should be the violet type with smaller cloves and, some people maintain, a more delicate flavour than the white garlic. The main point to remember is that, in a Provençal recipe which calls for one clove of garlic per person, the violet sort is meant; if you have only white garlic, allow three-quarters of a clove per person. The oil chosen is also very important: it must be olive oil. Of course, if you make your sauce with another kind of oil, it will look the same, but the flavour, indeed even the digestibility, can't compare with the real thing.

For 6	6 cloves of garlic
	1 yolk of egg
	250 ml (scant ½ pint; 1⅛ cups) olive oil
	salt, pepper
For 8–10	8–10 cloves of garlic
	2 yolks of egg
	500 ml (scant pint; 2¼ cups) olive oil
	salt, pepper

Remove any green shoots inside the garlic cloves, and reduce the cloves to a purée in a mortar. Add the egg yolk(s) and salt and pepper, and mix together. If you have taken the eggs out of the refrigerator, wait a minute or two for them to come up to room temperature: all the ingredients for a cold emulsion sauce should be at the same temperature to be certain of success.

Gradually pour on the olive oil, as for a mayonnaise, working it either with the pestle in the mortar or with a hand or electric whisk. The sauce should end up thick and firm. Taste and correct the seasoning. If you find that the garlic flavour is not strong enough, use a garlic press to squeeze out the last of each clove.

Anchoïade

Stronger than anchovy butter, anchoïade is a sauce, not a butter. In the south of France it is served as an appetizer, with slices of hot buttered toast, or with beautiful baskets full of raw vegetables of the season picked when ripe, such as tomatoes, violet artichokes, celery sticks, cauliflowers, radishes and cucumbers. In this recipe the butter is left out in favour of olive oil.

For 250 ml   250 g (8¾ oz) salted anchovies, or 125 g (4¼ oz)
(scant ½ pint;   anchovy fillets in oil
1⅛ cups)   2–3 cloves of garlic
sauce   1–2 tablespoons wine vinegar
        250 ml (scant ½ pint; 1⅛ cups) olive oil
        pepper from the mill

Skin the salted anchovies under the cold tap to obtain the fillets, without the bones. Leave them to soak for two hours in cold water, changing this several times. If you are using anchovy fillets in oil, add them as they are with their oil.

Put the anchovy fillets through the fine blade of the mincer or vegetable mill, together with the well-crushed garlic, and half the vinegar to rinse the blade. Then add the oil in a thin stream, as for a mayonnaise, beating with a wooden spoon. Season with pepper, taste and mix in the rest of the vinegar. It's a good idea to make the sauce an hour or two in advance of serving to give the flavours a chance to mellow and blend.

Anchovy butter

For 6   75 g (2½ oz) anchovy fillets
      1 small clove of garlic
      200 g (7 oz; ⅞ cup) fresh butter
      pepper

Soak the salted anchovy fillets in cold water to de-salt them, and wipe dry, or use tinned fillets in oil. Crush the anchovy fillets with the garlic in a mortar, and gradually incorporate the butter until you have a smooth paste. Then press through a fine-meshed sieve, using the pestle to get rid of any bits of anchovy. Season with pepper.

Put into a glass pot, or roll into a sausage-shape and wrap in greaseproof paper (don't use foil with anchovies). The butter will keep for several weeks, well-sealed, in the fridge. To serve hot, melt in a bain-marie, whisking all the time.

Barbecue sauce

This is one of the best home-made sauces that I have tasted. It is a wonderful accompaniment to American spareribs (pork chops cut on the cross), to everything cooked over charcoal—chicken pieces, whole chicken on the spit, or fish—and to meat fondue. As the sauce keeps for a long time in the refrigerator, you can easily make it in advance.

For 750 ml	3 medium onions
(1¼ pints;	5 tablespoons olive oil
3¼ cups)	200g (7 oz; ⅞ cup) tomato concentrate
sauce	4 tablespoons cider vinegar
	5 tablespoons white wine or degreased bouillon
	5 tablespoons Worcester sauce
	1 teaspoon thyme leaves
	1 bayleaf
	2 cloves of garlic
	4 tablespoons honey
	1 heaped teaspoon strong mustard
	5 leaves of mint or basil
	salt, pepper, cayenne pepper, Tabasco sauce (optional)

Heat the oil in a thick-bottomed saucepan, put in the finely chopped onions and soften. When they begin to colour, add the tomato concentrate, thinned with the vinegar. Bring to the boil and cook for two minutes, then add the wine or bouillon and Worcester sauce, followed by the thyme, bayleaf, crushed garlic, honey, mustard and bruised mint or basil leaves. Leave to simmer uncovered over a gentle heat for about fifteen minutes, until the sauce is creamy.

Taste, season with salt and pepper, and mix in a tiny dash of cayenne to pep it up. Turn off the heat, cover the pan and allow to cool. When you come to serve the sauce, hot or cold, taste it again and, if it doesn't seem piquant enough, carefully add a few drops of Tabasco. This is a pimento essence from the West Indies, and can be bought in small bottles.

Béarnaise sauce

For 6
1 tablespoon white tarragon vinegar
5 shallots
2 tablespoons tarragon leaves
3 yolks of egg
250 g (8¾ oz; 1⅛ cups) butter
1 tablespoon chopped chervil
salt, pepper

Over a fairly brisk heat, boil the vinegar with the finely chopped shallots and half the tarragon, until the liquid has evaporated. Leave to cool.

Put the shallots in the top of a bain-marie, add the egg yolks, 2 tablespoons cold water and salt and pepper. Heat gently, as for a hollandaise sauce, beating in the butter in pieces. At the point of serving, check the seasoning and add the rest of the tarragon and the chervil.

For this type of sauce, which requires great care to succeed, you need to keep an eye on the heat of the bain-marie: the water in the bottom should never boil. If, in addition, you mix a half-teaspoon of flour (no more) into the egg yolks, the emulsion will be less fragile.

Béchamel sauce

Béchamel sauce is one of the most useful: it is the basis of so many preparations that the housewife should always have some in reserve in the refrigerator, kept as a thickened sauce but not seasoned. It is an equally good foundation for both sweet and savoury soufflés or for confectioner's custard. Thinned a little, it is a creamy, velvety sauce; enriched with cheese it becomes Mornay sauce; lightened still further, it can be a creamy white sauce; seasoned with lemon juice and mushrooms, or, with egg yolks, a velouté sauce. Its uses are numerous, ranging from cod to gratin dishes, and going with the flavours of thyme, bayleaf, parsley, chervil, tarragon, chives, onion and many more.

BASIC BÉCHAMEL SAUCE

For 250 ml	1 tablespoon butter
(scant ½ pint;	2 level tablespoons flour
1⅛ cups)	250 ml (scant ½ pint; 1⅛ cups) cold boiled milk
sauce	salt, pepper, nutmeg

Melt the butter in a saucepan and, as soon as it begins to sizzle without browning, sprinkle with the flour. Work together thoroughly with a wooden spoon until the mixture starts to dry out and become crumbly, but still without colouring. Then pour in the milk all at once, stirring vigorously to prevent lumps forming. Heat to boiling point, stirring all the time, until large bubbles form, then turn down the heat and cook for 2 minutes, continuing to stir since the mixture sticks easily. Season with salt, pepper and nutmeg.

When the time comes to serve or use the sauce, add a good nut of butter, mixing it in so that it melts quickly: this will make your sauce glisten. You can also add a spoonful of thick cream which will intensify the smoothness and whiteness of the sauce.

CURRY SAUCE

Finely chop 100 g (3½ oz) onions and soften them in 15 g (½ oz; ¹⁄₁₆ cup) butter over a very gentle heat without browning. Sprinkle with 1 tablespoon curry powder, mix in and at once pour in the basic béchamel, which should not be too thick. Cook over a brisk heat stirring all the time, and when the sauce is nice and smooth, strain it through a fine-meshed sieve. Return to the pan, reheat and check the seasoning, which should be fairly spicy. Finish with another 15 g (½ oz; ¹⁄₁₆ cup) butter. For eggs, chicken, fish, smoked haddock.

LEMON SAUCE

Lighten the basic béchamel with 125 g (4¼ oz; ½ cup) thick cream, 1 yolk of egg and 2 teaspoons lemon juice. For poultry and veal offal, and fish with flesh of a solid texture.

MORNAY SAUCE

Before seasoning the basic béchamel, add 2–3 tablespoons grated Gruyère cheese and, if you like a strong cheese flavour, 1 tablespoon Parmesan. Season with salt and pepper right at the end and grind over some nutmeg to heighten the flavour. For eggs, gratin dishes, veal, chicken.

MUSHROOM SAUCE

Finely chop 150 g (5¼ oz) button mushrooms and sprinkle with lemon juice to keep them white. Cook in a nut of butter until they have released their moisture and this has evaporated, then add to the basic béchamel. For gratin dishes, thickening gravies, etc.

WHITE CREAM SAUCE

To the basic béchamel, add 3–4 tablespoons pouring cream (in France, 'fleurette' would be used, which has less fat content and is thinner than double cream, similar to whipping cream). Cook the sauce for another minute or until it is the desired consistency—it should coat the spoon without sticking. Season with salt, pepper and nutmeg. For poached chicken, salt cod, smoked haddock.

Beurre blanc

This is the lightest of the emulsified or whisked-up sauces. Like hollandaise sauce, it is served warm, and will separate if kept too hot. Nevertheless, it is very easy to make successfully, and adds an incomparable delicacy to poached fish, both freshwater and from the sea, to scallops and to many fine vegetables like asparagus and artichokes.

For 6   300 g (10½ oz; 1⅜ cups) salted butter
4 tablespoons chopped shallots
8 tablespoons cider vinegar
4 tablespoons dry white wine, preferably Muscadet
the juice of 1 lemon
pepper

If at all possible, choose butter which is not pre-packed—the less refined the better. Using salted butter means that you don't have to salt the sauce and ensures that the seasoning is evenly distributed.

Take a round saucepan which is large enough to whisk in, and put in the shallots, vinegar and wine. Cook over a moderate heat until the liquid has evaporated and you are left with a creamy mass of shallots, being especially careful that the mixture does not stick or brown. Meanwhile, divide the butter, which should be fairly firm, into pieces the size of walnuts.

Still over a moderate heat, add 1 tablespoon of water to the shallots and heat without boiling. Then add 4–5 bits of the butter, of a consistency that can be picked up with your fingers, and whisk vigorously. As soon as the mixture is reduced to a cream, add some more pieces of butter and repeat the process. Continue until all the butter is incorporated, adding another tablespoon of water half way through. The most important thing is that the emulsion should never reach boiling point. Season with the lemon juice and pepper.

Bolognese sauce

This preparation is the basis for bolognese sauce, which is obtained by thinning the concentrate with degreased beef or poultry bouillon. It accompanies spaghetti and most Italian pasta like ravioli, canneloni and so on.

For 500 ml	200 g (7 oz) cooked ham
(scant pint;	150 g (5¼ oz) button mushrooms
2¼ cups)	2 onions
concentrated	1 clove of garlic
sauce	2 sticks of celery
	1 carrot
	500 g (1 lb 2 oz) tomatoes
	1 bayleaf, parsley
	thyme, 1 sprig of marjoram, or ¾ teaspoon each dried thyme and marjoram
	2 tablespoons olive oil
	200 g (7 oz) minced beef
	200 ml (⅓ pint; ⅞ cup) good quality red wine
	1 tablespoon flour
	salt, pepper, nutmeg
	1 dessertspoon grated Parmesan cheese
	a pinch of sugar (if necessary)

Finely chop the ham with its fat. Chop up the mushrooms, onions, garlic and celery together, and grate the carrot. Skin and de-seed the tomatoes. Tie together the bayleaf and parsley, and fresh thyme and marjoram if available, to make a bouquet garni.

In a heavy casserole, gently heat the oil, put in the ham and melt over a low heat. When it is beginning to colour, add the minced beef and, a few minutes later, the vegetables (excluding the tomatoes) and garlic. Brown lightly for 5 minutes, stirring so that all the ingredients are well heated, then pour in the wine. Allow to simmer, uncovered, over a low heat until the wine has evaporated, stirring occasionally.

Sprinkle with the flour, mix it in and brown slightly, then add the tomatoes and herbs. Season with salt, pepper and nutmeg, moisten with a few spoonfuls of water, and put the lid on the pan. Leave to simmer over a very gentle heat until the tomatoes have melted to form a thick, creamy mass with the other ingredients. Remove from the heat and, while still warm, add the Parmesan. Check the seasoning and, if the tomatoes have made it taste a little acid, add a pinch of sugar.

English-style Breadcrumbs

You will find two sorts of ready-made breadcrumbs in the shops—golden, used mainly for gratin dishes since they brown very quickly in the oven, and white. But the best white breadcrumbs are those you make yourself, with stale sandwich bread, crusts removed, put through the fine blade of the mincer. They can be used immediately, or left uncovered for twenty-four hours to dry and then kept in a tightly sealed glass jar. Breadcrumbing is simply coating the food with dry breadcrumbs, just before cooking if it is moist. But you can also use this recipe for filleted fish, deep- or shallow-fried, veal escalopes, meat balls and croquettes.

For at   100 g (3½ oz; ¾ cup) flour
least 6   2 eggs
              1 teaspoon oil
              salt, pepper
              150 g (5¼ oz) white breadcrumbs

Arrange three dishes in front of you, the first containing the flour, the second the eggs beaten with the salt and pepper and oil, the third the breadcrumbs. Dip the ingredients to be fried in the first two dishes in turn, shaking off the excess flour and egg after each coating, and finally in the third dish, pressing well so that the breadcrumbs stick. Fry at once in fat heated to just below smoking point to obtain a beautiful golden crust. For raw food like fish and escalopes, moderate the heat so that the food will both cook and turn golden in the same time. You can also coat the ingredients in advance and leave them on a board for 20–30 minutes; but you will have to dip them in the breadcrumbs once more just before cooking.

Green herb butter

This can be prepared in advance, working the butter together with aromatic herbs like parsley, chervil and chives, and keeping it in the refrigerator until ready for use. Fried meats, steaks, veal escalopes, boiled or sauté potatoes, French beans, are all enhanced by this butter.

For 125 g   2 tablespoons parsley
(4½ oz; ½ cup) 1 tablespoon chervil
herb butter   1 tablespoon chives
                   125 g (4¼ oz; ½ cup) salted butter

Finely chop the parsley and chervil, and cut up the chives with scissors. Dry the herbs by wringing gently in a cloth. Work them into the butter with a fork, then shape into a roll, wrap in foil and keep refrigerated.

You can make tarragon butter in the same way, using 3 tablespoons chopped tarragon leaves and a small pinch of fresh-ground pepper.

Hollandaise sauce

This is a mayonnaise made with butter, and the perfect example of a hot emulsified sauce. If it is easy to make successfully, it is difficult to keep hot, and the best you can do is stop it getting cold: have it waiting in a warm bain-marie and stir frequently. My advice is to prepare everything in advance, and actually make the sauce at the last minute.

For 6   3 yolks of egg
               2 tablespoons cider vinegar
               salt, pepper
               250 g (8¾ oz; 1⅛ cups) butter
               the juice of ½ lemon

Take a saucepan which will fit easily into a bain-marie. Have ready to hand a bowl of cold water so that you can quickly cool the bottom of the saucepan in case it becomes too hot. Squeeze the lemon and reserve the juice. Put the egg yolks, vinegar and salt and pepper into the saucepan, mix and set aside to wait. Meanwhile, cut the butter into lumps the size of plums; it should be cool rather than cold. All these operations can be done in advance.

Heat the water in the bottom of the bain-marie so that it is fairly hot—barely simmering or 'trembling' but never boiling. Put in the saucepan and begin stirring immediately, continuing throughout the whole process. Add a piece of butter, stir and, as soon as it has melted, add another, repeating until the emulsion has taken, at which point you can speed things up. If, at any stage, the sauce seems to be collapsing, this is because it is too hot: add a spoonful of iced water at once and place the saucepan in the bowl of cold water to cool it.

When all the butter has been absorbed, the sauce will have the consistency of a mayonnaise. Remove the saucepan from the bain-marie and continue to stir briskly until it has cooled a little. Taste and season with 1-2 teaspoons lemon juice, salt and pepper. Serve. For asparagus, add 3 tablespoons firmly whipped cream and you will have a chantilly sauce.

Mayonnaise

This is the model for cold emulsified sauces. It frightens beginners, but its secret is simple: it is essential that all the ingredients, and even the bowl, should be at room temperature. The proportions are 1 yolk of egg to 250 ml (scant ½ pint; 1⅛ cups) oil.

For 4–6   1 yolk of egg
               ½ teaspoon strong mustard
               salt, pepper
               vinegar or lemon juice
               250 ml (scant ½ pint; 1⅛ cups) oil

Take a bowl with a steady base, taller than it is wide, and put in the egg yolk, mustard, a little salt and pepper and 2–3 drops of vinegar or lemon juice. Mix together and leave for a minute or two, then begin stirring as you pour in the oil in a thin stream; you can use a wooden spoon, a hand whisk or an electric beater—it doesn't matter so long as the oil is incorporated quickly without leaving a ring and the mixture doesn't separate. Gradually increase the stream of oil and stir faster. The mayonnaise is ready when it is firm. Taste and add more vinegar and salt and pepper if necessary.

GREEN HERB MAYONNAISE
Chop very finely the following herbs, one after the other so that you can gauge how much is needed: 1 tablespoon each watercress leaves, chervil and parsley, 1–2 leaves of mint. Combine the herbs and add them by the spoonful to the mayonnaise. In principle their juices should lighten the mayonnaise but, if not, thin as indicated above.

MOUSSELINE MAYONNAISE
Whisk an egg white until it stands in firm peaks and add it gradually to the mayonnaise, folding it in without too much stirring.

PINK MAYONNAISE
The best pink mayonnaise is made with fresh, very red tomatoes. Skin and de-seed them, pound to a soft paste and season with a pinch of sweet red paprika. Add to the mayonnaise by the spoonful and check the seasoning. I can also recommend tomato concentrate, worked to a smooth paste with a pinch of spices. A little caster sugar and a dash of cayenne complete the seasoning.

SPICY MAYONNAISE
Incorporate a few drops of Tabasco sauce, or a pinch of cayenne pepper, or even a little hot pimento paste thinned with water or soya sauce. All these, used with caution, will add a pleasant piquancy.

THINNED MAYONNAISE
Add water, milk or pouring cream by the teaspoonful until you have the desired consistency.

Rouille

Rouille, related to aïoli, is a very spicy sauce of the consistency of mayonnaise, rust-coloured—whence the name—and much appreciated in Provence. It always accompanies bouillabaisse, as well as other homely fish soups, poached white fish and bourride, a savoury fish stew. While aïoli is simply garlic mayonnaise, the ingredients used in rouille are more controversial. Some people bulk it out and make it firmer with bread, soaked and squeezed dry, or with potatoes taken from the bouillabaisse and mashed while hot. It's good to know that you have nothing to fear from this little volcano: rich in pimentos and garlic, rouille is a powerful disinfectant of the digestive system and is welcome at any season.

For 6

2 cloves of garlic
2 small, hot, red pimentos, or 1 level teaspoon
     cayenne pepper
1 slice white sandwich bread
1 yolk of egg
a pinch of powdered saffron
salt
200 ml (⅓ pint; ⅞ cup) olive oil
2 tablespoons fish bouillon or bouillabaisse

Chop the pimentos and pound them in a mortar with the garlic until reduced to a cream. Add the bread, previously soaked and then squeezed into the shape of a small egg, and mix. Put in the egg yolk, a pinch of salt and the saffron, and then pour on the oil in a thin stream, beating to incorporate it as for a mayonnaise. Finally, thin the sauce by adding the fish soup or bouillon by the spoonful. Everyone helps themselves to the rouille, which is usually spread on rounds of bread which have been dried, but not toasted, in the oven, and adds them to their soup.

Snail butter

This butter is served not only with snails and shellfish, but also with frogs' legs, fried spring chicken, grilled or poached fish, wild mushrooms and cooked or raw vegetables. Make it the day before required; rolled into a sausage and wrapped in foil, it will keep for several days in the refrigerator, and the flavour will also improve.

For about	4 grey shallots
250 g (8¾ oz;	3–4 cloves of garlic
1⅛ cups)	parsley
snail butter	250g (8¾ oz; 1⅛ cups) fresh salted butter
	2 small leaves of dried sage (optional)
	½ teaspoon quatre-épices or mixed spices (pepper, cloves, nutmeg and ginger)
	white pepper from the mill

Finely chop the parsley—it should make 4 tablespoons. On a separate board, chop the shallots and garlic together and, if you have a mortar, pound them to a cream. Soften the butter, working it either with a fork on a board, or in an electric mixer, and at the same time incorporating the chopped shallots and garlic and parsley, the rubbed sage, spices and pepper.

Sorrel sauce

The principle of sorrel sauce is simple: it comes down to a handful of sorrel softened in butter and then incorporated in a sauce, which can be anything from plain cream to hollandaise, but is always specified in the recipes where it is required. This is the sauce for fish, poached as well as baked, for scallops, poached eggs, fried veal escalopes and other dishes.

For 250 ml	250 g (8¾ oz) sorrel leaves
(scant ½ pint;	30 g (1 oz; ⅛ cup) butter
1⅛ cups)	250 g (8¾ oz; 1 cup) pouring cream or double cream
sorrel sauce	salt, pepper

Pick over the sorrel and remove the stalks as far as the middle of the leaves. Wash and dry them and cut roughly into strips. Soften in a saucepan with the butter, stirring so that it is quickly reduced to a cream and retains its colour as much as possible.

If you are using pouring cream, which is preferable since it thickens quickly after boiling, pour it all at once onto the sorrel and bring to the boil, stirring all the time. As soon as the sauce coats the spoon, remove the pan from the heat and season with salt and pepper. If you can only get double cream, bring it to the boil in a separate pan. When it is thick enough to coat the spoon, pour it onto the sorrel, cook for another half minute and season with salt and pepper.

This sauce is not fussy, and can be kept in a cool place and reheated without difficulty when required. You can also add the sorrel base to a hollandaise sauce, providing they are both at the same temperature, and this is the sauce for fine, large, poached fish like bass, pike, perch and even cod and its relatives. It is served in a sauceboat, sprinkled with chervil leaves.

Tapénade

This is a seasoned anchovy paste which is specifically Provençal. (The name comes from tapéno—Provençal for capers.) It is eaten spread on small slices of brown bread with an aperitif, or with hard-boiled eggs as an hors d'oeuvre, or as one of the accompaniments to a stockpot. It can be kept in little glass jars in a cool place.

> 3 cloves of garlic
> 200 g (7 oz) black olives
> 1 small tin of anchovy fillets in oil
> the yolks of 3 hard-boiled eggs
> 1 small tin of tuna fish
> a pinch of thyme leaves
> 1–2 tablespoons pickled capers
> olive oil
> pepper
> lemon juice

Begin by crushing the garlic cloves in a mortar. Remove and reserve so that you can add as much as necessary later on—the paste should not be dominated by garlic. Stone the olives and pound them in the mortar with the anchovies and their oil, the egg yolks, the tuna drained of its juices, the thyme and half the garlic. When all these ingredients are blended to a paste, add about a third of their volume in capers. Then reduce to a smooth paste, taste and decide if the rest of the garlic is required.

Pour on the oil in a thin stream, stirring all the time. Season with pepper and squeeze in a few drops of lemon juice. You should have a smooth, soft paste which, after chilling for at least an hour, should firm to the consistency of butter. If you don't have a mortar, you can make the tapénade using the fine blade of the mincer or vegetable mill, or an electric mixer or blender.

Tartare sauce

This is a mayonnaise made from hard-boiled egg yolks, and is flavoured with finely chopped spring onions, gherkins, chives and capers. It is preferred to ordinary mayonnaise for lobster and other crustaceans, large fish served cold, seafood salads, hard-boiled eggs and other dishes.

For 6
2 yolks of hard-boiled egg
½ teaspoon strong mustard
wine or cider vinegar
250 ml (scant ½ pint; 1⅛ cup) groundnut oil
1 tablespoon chives or chervil
1 tablespoon spring onions or white onions
1 tablespoon pickled gherkins
½ tablespoon small capers
salt, pepper

Crush the egg yolks to a purée with the mustard, season lightly with salt and pepper, and thin with a few drops of vinegar. Leave to rest for 2–3 minutes, and meanwhile cut up the chives or chervil with scissors and finely chop the onions and gherkins.

Pour on the oil in a thin stream, stirring with a whisk or wooden spoon—it doesn't matter which as long as the sauce amalgamates quickly. Thin occasionally with a few drops of vinegar if the mixture becomes too solid. Finish by adding the rest of the ingredients a little at a time, taste and correct the seasoning if necessary.

Tomato sauce

This 'coulis' and ordinary tomato sauce have the same uses. However, this is more concentrated because of the amount of cooking, and is served on its own, whereas the basic sauce is usually added to a dish during cooking as a moistening and flavouring agent.

For 500 ml	2 onions
(scant pint;	3 cloves of garlic
2¼ cups)	2 sticks of celery
thick tomato	2 carrots
sauce	50 g (1¾ oz; ¼ cup) butter or olive oil
	1 kg (2 lb 4 oz) tomatoes
	1 bouquet garni, with thyme predominating
	salt, pepper
	sugar, if necessary
	cayenne pepper (optional)
	tarragon, basil or fines herbes, according to choice

Chop the onions, garlic and celery and grate the carrots. Cook them without colouring in the butter or oil in a saucepan. Skin and de-seed the tomatoes, and crush them to get rid of the juice. When the mixture in the pan is softened, add the tomatoes and bouquet garni, cover the pan and simmer until the tomatoes have melted to a creamy mass. Take off the lid, and continue cooking until the sauce is the desired consistency. Discard the bouquet garni, strain the sauce and season with salt and pepper. For a piquant flavour, add a dash of cayenne, but if the sauce tastes acid, sweeten with a sugar lump or 1 teaspoon caster sugar. Finish the sauce with the chosen herb just before serving.

Vinaigrette

This sauce is made with oil and vinegar, salt, pepper, mustard and various aromatics, and is one of the most common in cookery. It is a dressing for salads—from green salad to warm or cold potato salad—for vegetables, fish and shellfish and other food. In some countries vinaigrette is sweetened with sugar, in others the dressing is often pepped up with Worcester or other spicy sauces.

The quality of the vinaigrette is entirely dependent on that of its ingredients: the oil—olive, walnut, groundnut or corn—and the vinegar—wine, cider, sherry, or wine vinegar flavoured with fruit like raspberries (ordinary white vinegar is only used for pickling things like gherkins and onions). The proportions are 4 tablespoons oil, salt and pepper, to 1 tablespoon, or a little less, vinegar. If adding mustard, do so with caution—½ teaspoon.

Dieticians advise that you should always pour the oil onto the salt and pepper before adding the vinegar: salt acts directly with vinegar to increase its acidity. In fact this mixture is used to clean copper and brass.

Soups

American vichyssoise

This iced soup is served in cups, and the bite of the chives or spring onions adds to the pleasure.

For 6
4 medium leeks
2 onions
5 medium potatoes
40 g (1½ oz; generous ⅛ cup) butter
1 litre (1¾ pints; 4½ cups) chicken stock
150 g (5¼ oz; ⅝ cup) fresh cream
chives, spring onions, chervil
salt, pepper

Roughly chop the white part of the leeks and the onions. Slice the potatoes into rounds. Soften the leeks and onions, without colouring, in the butter and, when they have become transparent, add the potatoes. Cook gently, stirring all the time, for 3–4 minutes, so that the potatoes become impregnated with butter and their moisture evaporates—all of which helps to improve the flavour. Heat the stock to boiling in a separate pan, then add to the vegetables, put on the lid and leave to cook gently until the potatoes are soft.

Process in the liquidizer and press through a fine-meshed sieve, so that the soup is velvety-smooth and there are no lumps. Allow to cool, mix in the cream, and season with salt and pepper from the mill. Refrigerate.

When you come to serve the soup, add some ice cubes—it doesn't matter if these are poured into the cups along with the soup. It is only at this stage that you can judge the consistency of the soup, which should be very smooth, not pasty. Finish by decorating with spring herbs like chervil and chives or spring onions.

Avocado cream soup

This soup, which should be served in cups, is bound to win over those who don't normally like avocados. It is made in the liquidizer and served cold. Since it is a last-minute soup, you will have to warn your guests: its beautiful pale green colour will be spoilt if kept waiting too long.

For 4   500 ml (scant pint; 2¼ cups) chicken stock
2 avocados
1 lemon
1 tablespoon fresh dill, or 1 teaspoon powdered dill
½ teaspoon powdered or dehydrated onion
2 tablespoons dry sherry
100 g (3½ oz; ⅜ cup) fresh cream
salt, pepper

First make the chicken stock by dissolving a stock cube in a little hot water, then topping up with cold water to obtain the right amount. Peel and cut up the avocados, rubbing with lemon juice as you go so that they don't turn black. Put them in the liquidizer with half the bouillon, the powdered dill (the fresh is added later) and onion, and blend to a thick, very smooth cream.

Pour into a glass or china bowl and, to finish the soup, mix in the sherry, cream and rest of the stock, and season with salt and pepper. Check the seasoning, and now add the fresh dill, if you are using it, cut up with scissors. Put the soup into the freezer for a few minutes, to chill not freeze it, or chill by adding some ice cubes.

Broad bean soup from the Languedoc

This is more than a soup; it is a sumptuous and complete meal. An example of regional home cooking, it comes from Gascony, the land of preserved goose, Armagnac and foie gras. All the meat used is preserved goose or duck, or a mixture of the two; the broad beans, small, young and delicate, are cooked in their skins; and the 'farci', a sort of thick, fried pancake, finishes up in the liquid. The combination of these rich ingredients could be indigestible without the hyssop, but this acts as an effective stimulant. It also gives a flavour which you will want to incorporate in many other substantial and fatty dishes.

For 6–8

THE SOUP

3 kg (6 lb 12 oz) young, spring broad beans
2–3 cloves of garlic
4 large onions, or 12 small white onions
butter or oil
1 wing or 1 leg of preserved goose, or 6 whole legs of preserved duck
1 large bouquet garni: parsley, thyme, bayleaf
1 head of celery, or 1 bunch of celery leaves
6 large whole chives tied together
2 sprigs of fresh hyssop, or 1 tablespoon dried hyssop leaves
salt, pepper, sugar

THE FARCI

3 poultry livers with the hearts
300 g (10½ oz) belly pork
2 gizzards of preserved goose or duck
4 shallots
1 large tablespoon parsley
1 small bowl of dried breadcrumbs
3–4 eggs, according to size
salt, pepper, sugar

Shell the broad beans—you should have about 1 kg (2 lb 4 oz) shelled beans. Bring to the boil 3 litres (5¼ pints; 6½ US pints) water, seasoned with salt and 1 teaspoon sugar, put in the beans and turn down the heat. Meanwhile, chop the onions and garlic, and soften them in a little butter or oil in a frying pan, over a moderate heat so that they don't brown. Place the goose or duck pieces on a grid in a roasting pan and quickly heat in the oven, so that they release their fat without actually roasting. Reserve the fat for the farci.

Add the softened onions and garlic to the broad beans and water, together with the bouquet garni, celery and herbs, and the goose or duck. Cook gently for 45 minutes, then remove from the heat, cover the pan and set aside.

To make the farci, finely chop the livers, hearts and pork, and the gizzards stripped of their hard skin. Chop the shallots and parsley. Mix all the ingredients, including the eggs and breadcrumbs, in a bowl, and season with salt and pepper and a pinch of sugar.

Melt a good tablespoonful of the reserved goose or duck fat in a frying pan. Cook the farci like a thick omelette and, when it is firm, fold it over in three (bringing the two sides to the middle) and then turn it over to seal the join with the heat.

Skim the fat from the soup and season with salt and pepper. Reheat it and, when the liquid is barely simmering, carefully slide in the farci without breaking it. Poach without boiling for 25–30 minutes.

To serve, slice the farci and divide between the dishes; share out the goose or duck, and cover with the soup and broad beans, after removing the bouquet garni. Serve some toasted crusty bread at the same time.

Later in the season, when broad beans are mature, you will need to strip them of the bitter skins by blanching for a few minutes in boiling water. They also have a tendency to disintegrate to a purée, so it is better to add them to the soup half way through the cooking, and to make sure that it doesn't boil too furiously. In the winter, you can use white haricot beans instead of broad beans, first soaked for 2 hours in warm water.

Cabbage soup with Roquefort

Cabbage is so rich in vitamins and trace elements that it can be considered in the same category as culinary herbs in a well-planned diet. The original touch of this excellent soup is the velvety flavour of the Roquefort cheese, which is added to the soup bowls.

For 6   300 g (10½ oz) mild, salt belly pork, or unsmoked
                      streaky bacon
               4 carrots
               1 onion
               cloves
               1 small Savoy cabbage
               2 leeks
               3 potatoes
               salt, pepper
               crusty white bread
               200 g (7 oz) Roquefort cheese

Wash and pat dry the salt pork or bacon, and cut into large sticks. Put into 2 litres (3½ pints; 4½ US pints) cold water, bring to the boil and skim. Leave to cook for 30 minutes. Then add the carrots, cut into small sticks or cubes, and the onion stuck with a clove or two.

Meanwhile, cut the cabbage into quarters and blanch for 10 minutes in boiling water without allowing it to break up. Refresh in cold water and cut into fine strips, discarding the large ribs. Add to the soup, bring back to the boil and cook steadily for 30 minutes. Then add the sliced white part of the leeks and the potatoes cut into large cubes (as if for sautéeing). After 2 hours, the soup will be cooked, although it can be kept waiting. Season with salt and pepper, remembering that the cheese is salty; and if the liquid has reduced too much, thin with boiling water.

Serve with the bread. Each person puts a few slices in his soup bowl with a piece of Roquefort the size of a large sugar lump; the hot soup is ladled on and the cheese melts.

Gazpacho

A salad turned into a soup, a wonderful creamy mixture of raw vegetables, served iced.

For 6   1 kg (2 lb 4 oz) tomatoes
            200 g (7 oz) stale white bread, crusts removed
            ½ cucumber
            1 small, sweet red pepper
            2 small white onions
            4 tablespoons olive oil
            2 tablespoons vinegar
            1 clove of garlic
            salt
            fried bread cubes

Plunge the tomatoes into boiling water to skin them. De-seed them and cut the flesh into tiny bits. Soak the bread in water and then squeeze dry. Peel the half-cucumber, remove the seeds and cut into very fine dice, and the sweet pepper as well. Slice the onions thinly.

Put the tomatoes and bread into the liquidizer to make a thin, soft paste. Add the oil, vinegar, salt, crushed garlic, 2 tablespoons diced cucumber and half the sweet pepper, and reduce to a cream with

750 ml (1¼ pints; 3¼ cups) water. Turn into a bowl and keep in the refrigerator or a cold place for 2–3 hours.

To serve, add a tray of ice cubes to the soup, and have on the table small bowls containing the onions, the rest of the cucumber and sweet pepper, and small cubes of bread fried in oil. If you don't like bits of raw vegetable you can drink the soup as it is, while others can help themselves to the garnish. Serve the gazpacho in cups.

Pistou soup

This is a soup of the Nice region of France, with a beautiful scent of basil. It is known throughout Provence simply as pistou. Every family has their own method of making it, some adding pasta, others scornfully dismissing the idea, but the basic ingredients are the same. It is from a famous cook of Nice, Jeanine Raibaud-Dumas, that I have borrowed this recipe.

For 6–8   THE SOUP
200 g (7 oz) white haricot beans, either fresh and shelled, or dried and soaked
500 g (1 lb 2 oz) potatoes
4 medium carrots
200 g (7 oz) plump French or pod beans
3 medium leeks
4 medium courgettes (squash)
3 medium tomatoes
125 g (4¼ oz) rolled salt belly pork (from an Italian delicatessen)
200 g (7 oz) shelled peas, fresh or frozen
salt, pepper

THE PISTOU
1 bunch of basil, or 15 large leaves
2 cloves of garlic
50 g (1¾ oz) grated Gruyère cheese
1 tablespoon grated Parmesan cheese (optional)
olive oil

Shell the fresh white haricot beans or, if using dried ones, soak them in cold water until well swollen and then weigh out the correct amount. Cut the potatoes and carrots into dice. Slice the beans into lengths of about 1 cm (½ in), and do the same with the white part of the leeks. Do not peel the courgettes, but cut them into rounds 1 cm (½ in) thick. Skin and de-seed the tomatoes. Cut the salt pork into small sticks.

Put the potatoes, carrots, haricot beans, green beans and leeks into a stockpot with 3 litres (5¼ pints; 6½ US pints) water. Bring to the boil for 10 minutes, then add the salt pork, courgettes, tomatoes and peas, and lower the heat. Cook gently for 2 hours. At this stage, stir the soup with a fork to separate the ingredients without breaking up the vegetables, and season lightly with salt.

While the soup is cooking, prepare the pistou. Put the basil leaves and garlic cloves into a wooden or marble mortar, and crush to a pulp. Then add the cheese by the spoonful, moistening with a little oil, until you have a smooth paste, soft but not runny.

Add the pistou to the hot soup, off the fire, and stir it in. Season with pepper and taste to check the seasoning, then bring to the boil once and serve immediately.

Sorrel and chervil cream soup

Quickly made and delicious, this is one of the best soups for any season. The chervil leaves add the finishing touch and heighten the flavours.

For 6   1 large handful of sorrel leaves
40 g (1½ oz; generous ⅛ cup) butter
1 tablespoon flour
2–3 medium potatoes
100 g (3½ oz; ⅜ cup) cream
1 bunch of chervil
1 yolk of egg
salt
toast cubes

Pick over the sorrel leaves, removing the stalks and large ribs. Set aside 4–5 leaves for later and chop the rest roughly. Melt the butter in a large saucepan and put in the sorrel. When it is softened, sprinkle with the flour, stir to mix and pour on 2 litres (3½ pints; 4½ US pints) water. Add the potatoes, cut into cubes or thin rounds, and cook briskly until the potatoes are done.

Meanwhile, cut up the chervil coarsely with scissors or pick off the leaves by hand. Put in the bottom of the soup tureen with the egg yolk and leave to macerate for at least 10 minutes. Cut the reserved sorrel leaves into fine strips. Process the soup in the vegetable mill or liquidizer, return to the pan and reheat. Then add the shredded sorrel and the cream, and immediately take off the heat. Season with salt and pour gradually into the tureen, stirring quickly. Serve small cubes of toast separately.

You can equally well substitute brown rice for the potatoes, but then there is no need for the flour.

Tourin of Lavaur

Tourin is a soup of south-western France, with recipes varying in different areas. This is one of the sturdier versions, which I found in Lavaur. It used to be served to hunters on a frosty morning and, according to the lady of the house, put wings on their feet and brought roses to their cheeks!

For 6   8–15 cloves of garlic
stale, crusty white bread
2 eggs
200 g (7 oz) olive oil
salt, pepper

Peel the garlic cloves and reduce to a cream, either in a mortar, using 8–10 cloves, or with a garlic press, using all 15. Place in the bottom of a soup tureen and cover with 2 layers of bread slices. Put on the lid and leave for the flavours to blend.

Separate the yolks and whites of the eggs. Pour the olive oil in a thin stream on to the yolks, stirring all the time, to make a mayonnaise. Heat 200 ml (⅓ pint; ⅞ cup) salted water in a saucepan and, when it is boiling steadily, add the egg whites. As soon as they have formed, remove the pan from the heat. Thin the mayonnaise with a few spoonfuls of the boiling water, added one at a time and mixed in, and then, still off the heat, add the mayonnaise to the pan. Mix, taste, season with pepper, and pour into the soup tureen. Put on the lid, leave for 5–8 minutes to draw out the flavours, and serve.

Vegetable soup

All the vegetables for this soup are cut into fine dice and softened in butter or goose fat to heighten the flavours. Chicken giblets, wings and feet are used to give body to the stock, although they don't appear in the final dish.

For 6   giblets from 2 chickens, including wings, neck,
                        gizzard and feet, or whole carcase of 1 chicken
                   300 g (10½ oz) carrots
                   100 g (3½ oz) turnips
                   300 g (10½ oz) potatoes
                   3 medium leeks
                   1 head of celery
                   60 g (2 oz; ¼ cup) butter, or 30 g (1 oz; ⅛ cup) goose
                        fat
                   salt, pepper
                   parsley
                   1 yolk of egg

Ask your poulterer for the chicken giblets and perhaps a couple of extra feet, and blanch them in boiling water. Skin the feet, removing the claws, and tie them together. Put all in the stockpot with 2 litres (3½ pints; 4½ US pints) water, a little salt and 4 peppercorns. Poach until completely cooked.

Meanwhile, cut all the vegetables into small dice, using only the white part of the leeks; make sure you have chosen potatoes which don't disintegrate during cooking. Sweat them in half the butter or all the goose fat over a moderate heat without colouring. Then add to the stock and cook steadily for 30–40 minutes. When the carrots are cooked, the soup is ready.

Discard the chicken giblets and check the seasoning. If the stock has reduced too much, thin with boiling water before seasoning. Just before serving, add the rest of the butter; if you have been cooking with goose fat, there is no need to add more at this stage, as its fat content is higher than that of butter. Put 2 tablespoons finely chopped parsley and the yolk of egg in the bottom of the soup tureen. Leave for the flavours to blend for 10–15 minutes. Then slowly pour on the hot soup, stirring all the time, and serve.

Starters, Salads, Eggs and Pasta

Artichokes au gratin

This dish is made with artichoke hearts, stripped of the leaves, rubbed with lemon, cooked in salted water, and then filled with a béchamel sauce incorporating chopped ham, Gruyère and Parmesan. You can use tinned or frozen hearts, and prepare it in advance.

For 6
6 large artichokes, or tinned or frozen hearts
2 lemons
750 ml (1¼ pints; 3¼ cups) béchamel sauce (see p. 52)
180 g (6¼ oz) cooked ham
100 g (3½ oz) Gruyère cheese
40 g (1½ oz) Parmesan cheese
salt, pepper, nutmeg

If using whole, fresh artichokes, prepare each one by breaking off the stalk level with the base (don't cut it). With a very sharp knife, cut back the large outer leaves to the edible parts, and slice all round the base, removing the hard bits. Rub with lemon juice as you go—artichokes quickly turn black. Cut off the small inner leaves and scoop out the choke with a sharp round spoon.

Cook the hearts in boiling salted water, with lemon juice added. Test to see when they are done with the blade of a knife, which should slip easily into a heart. Meanwhile, prepare the béchamel sauce, incorporate the chopped ham and grated cheese, and season fairly highly with salt, pepper and nutmeg. Preheat the oven to 230°C/450°F/Mark 8, if you are intending to cook the gratin now.

Drain the cooked artichoke hearts, and arrange them, concave side up, on a hot gratin dish. Cover with the sauce and place in the hot oven. Watch that the surface does not brown too quickly, before the dish is bubbling.

You can prepare this dish the day before, or a few hours in advance, up to the stage where it is ready to go into the oven. When the time comes to cook it, adjust the oven temperature so that the dish is completely heated through before the top browns.

Artichokes vinaigrette

Always choose artichokes with the leaves intact; if they are no longer fresh, artichokes start to ferment and, because of the gas produced, can become indigestible. They are sold with the stalks attached, and this should be pulled off, not cut, in order to remove the hard threads which spoil the quality of the heart. Allow one artichoke per person.

For 6   6 artichokes
               salt
               vinaigrette (see p.64)

Take a large saucepan which will hold the artichokes with plenty of room, fill it with water and bring to the boil. Trim the artichokes by removing the tips of the green leaves and paring round with a knife down to the first edible leaves. Cook them in the boiling water—you can tell when they are done by pulling off a large leaf, which should come away easily but firmly. You can now serve them as they are, but it is better to prepare them as follows.

Spread out the green leaves surrounding the core of small violet leaves, and lift out this central part in one. Scoop out the choke with a soup spoon, and replace the lid of violet leaves to cover the hole. Serve with the vinaigrette in a bowl on the table, so that everyone can help themselves.

For a delicate hors d'oeuvre, serve with hollandaise, béarnaise or mousseline sauce, or white cream sauce. In this case, fill the heart with a good tablespoonful of the sauce before replacing the lid, and hand the rest of the sauce round in a sauceboat.

Asparagus

It is difficult to leave out this delicious vegetable in a collection of recipes, despite its short spring season. The green type has its followers, although the white is more widespread. The cooking of asparagus demands some care, but at table it is quite happy accompanied by hollandaise or mousseline sauce (see p. 57) lightened with beaten egg whites or whipped cream) when hot, or by vinaigrette or frothy mayonnaise when cold. In the preparation of asparagus it is most important to scrape the stalks thoroughly and cook them well.

For 6   2.5–3 kg (5 lb 10 oz–6 lb 12 oz) asparagus
            salt

Scrape the asparagus stalks with a vegetable knife, working from the base to the tip and removing any hard outside bits, depending on how fresh they are. Cut off the tough base of the stalks and trim them to more or less the same length. Wash them and tie together in bundles, not too many at once—although this may sound fussy, it is important for presentation.

Take a fairly long pan—a large oval casserole dish is often the best— and arrange the asparagus in it without crowding the tips. Cover with boiling water, season with salt, put the lid on and cook steadily but gently. After 20 minutes, test one of the large stalks with the point of a knife: it should be firm, not hard, but be careful—over-cooked asparagus hangs its head in shame.

Now you will appreciate the usefulness of tying the asparagus with string. Lift out the bundles with a fork and place them whole on a long dish lined with a napkin. Leave them to cool a little, then remove the string and serve with the chosen sauce.

Aubergine (egg plant) caviar

This is an hors d'oeuvre which is eaten in Russia, but which could be called Slav since it is found as far afield as the Balkans, based on the same ingredients, ranging from coarse to smooth, and served with sour black bread.

For 6   3–4 very fresh aubergines (egg plant)
            1 very firm tomato
            2–3 small white onions
            1–2 cloves of garlic
            1 tablespoon chopped dill, or 1 teaspoon powdered
                dill, or very finely chopped parsley
            1 glass olive oil
            8–10 coriander seeds
            lemon juice (optional)
            salt, pepper

Choose long aubergines, which usually contain fewer seeds, and cut off the stalks. Put them whole into a hot oven, at least 180°/350°F/ Mark 4–5, and cook until the skin is dry and cracked and they are soft to the touch. Blanch the tomato in boiling water to skin it, then cut open on the cross, de-seed it and squeeze gently to remove excess moisture. Peel the aubergines and put through the fine blade of the mincer or vegetable mill together with the tomato flesh. Crush the onions and garlic in the garlic press.

Put all the prepared ingredients in a bowl with the dill or parsley, and mix. Pour on the oil in a thin stream, stirring vigorously with a wooden spoon, as for a mayonnaise. Season with salt, pepper, and the coriander seeds, crushed in the peppermill or with a mallet. Taste and sharpen with a few drops of lemon juice if necessary. Serve chilled with black bread or toasted crusty white bread and butter.

Gratin of courgettes (squash) with rice

The uncooked rice sprinkled over the precooked courgettes absorbs their moisture, while the surface becomes crisp and golden. This is one of those dishes which is equally good hot or cold.

For 6
2 kg (4 lb 8 oz) courgettes (squash)
3 tablespoons brown rice
3 eggs
250 g (8¾ oz; 1 cup) cream
200 g (7 oz) Mimolette, Edam or Gouda cheese
salt, pepper

Peel the courgettes and slice into thick rounds. Add to 3 litres (5¼ pints; 6½ US pints) boiling salted water, and cook steadily for about 10 minutes or until the courgettes are tender. Turn into a colander and drain thoroughly, pressing gently with the back of a spoon.

Preheat the oven to 180°C/350°F/Mark 4. Arrange the courgettes in a gratin dish and scatter the rice over the top. Beat the eggs with the cream and grated cheese, and season with pepper followed by salt (adjust the amount depending on the saltiness of the cheese). Pour over the courgettes, lifting them slightly with a fork so that the mixture is evenly distributed. Bake in the oven for 40 minutes, so that the rice is cooked while absorbing the rest of the moisture from the courgettes, and the surface is lightly browned. The brown rice acts as a thickener and is scarcely noticeable in the finished dish, although it has absorbed the excess liquid from the courgettes.

Cucumbers with cream

A refreshing salad which can be part of a mixed hors d'oeuvre.

For 6   2 cucumbers
10 sprigs of tarragon
2 lemons
200 g (7 oz; ¾ cup) fresh cream
salt, pepper

Choose very firm cucumbers, wash and wipe them. Without peeling, slice into rounds as thin as possible, using the special blade of a cheese grater. Put in a colander, sprinkle generously with table salt, stir and leave for 30 minutes to extract the juices.

Rinse the cucumbers in cold water, stirring them around, drain and pat dry. Place in a bowl with the chopped tarragon leaves, and season with pepper and the juice of 1 lemon. Keep in a cool place. Just before serving, add the cream by the spoonful, stirring until all the slices are coated. Taste, and, if necessary, add more lemon juice and cream, but not too much. Serve in individual glass bowls or a salad bowl, trimmed with small bunches of tarragon.

Marinated sweet peppers

These peeled sweet peppers in olive oil will keep, sealed from the air and refrigerated, for several weeks, and can be used as an hors d'oeuvre or to flavour other dishes. When fresh basil is available, use it to scent the olive oil—this will add a delicate touch.

                1 kg (2 lb 4 oz) large sweet peppers, red or green
2 glasses olive oil
2 cloves of garlic
salt, pepper

Heat up the grill for 15 minutes, leaving the door open if it is an oven grill. Brush the sweet peppers with oil, place on a grid (half way up if in the oven) and grill, turning them so that the skin is blackened

all over and will come away easily. To make them easier to skin, wrap
the peppers, as soon as they are grilled, in several thicknesses of
paper or in a damp cloth, and leave for 10 minutes. When you unwrap
them, the skin can be peeled off without difficulty.

Cut them in half lengthwise and remove the seeds. Cut into wide
strips, lay flat in a bowl, season with salt and pepper, and squeeze the
garlic over the surface with a garlic press. Cover with the olive oil,
cover the bowl and leave to marinate for at least 24 hours in a cool
place, but not in the refrigerator. Serve as an hors d'oeuvre with
salads or anchovy fillets in oil, or add to ratatouilles, dishes 'à la
basquaise' and mixed salads.

Brain fritters

This starter can be prepared several hours in advance, and the final
frying done just before serving.

For 6   6–8 lambs' brains
2 tablespoons finely chopped parsley
1 lemon
1 tablespoon oil
salt, pepper
oil for frying

THE BATTER
100 g (3½ oz; ¾ cup) flour
a pinch of salt
1 tablespoon oil
2 whites of egg

If you are using fresh brains, soak them for 1 hour in very cold
water to remove all traces of blood. Frozen brains can be used as they
are, without defrosting. Poach the brains in boiling water, strongly
seasoned with salt and pepper, for 10 minutes. Drain and leave to
cool a little and firm. Then cut each lobe in two, arrange in a dish and
scatter with the parsley. Sprinkle with the lemon juice mixed with the
oil, and set aside to marinate in a cool place for 30 minutes.

Prepare the frying batter just before required. Sift the flour into a
bowl, make a well in the centre and add the salt and oil. Mix quickly,
but without working too hard, with just enough warm water to obtain

a smooth, slightly thick paste. If there are any lumps, you will have to strain it, rather than beating, to get rid of them. Whisk the egg whites to a firm snow and fold them in, taking up the mixture without stirring or beating it.

Heat the frying oil until hot but not smoking. Take the brains out of the marinade and pat them dry, leaving the parsley sticking. With a fork, dip them into the batter and immediately place in the hot oil, so that they swell and firm without colouring. Remove the fritters from the oil and drain. They can be kept waiting for the final operation.

Just before serving, reheat the frying oil until it is just beginning to smoke. Put the fritters in a frying basket and plunge into the hot oil long enough for them to turn a pale golden colour; this is the secret of crisp fritters. Sprinkle with a little salt and serve in a napkin, accompanied by a highly seasoned, hot tomato sauce or a cold tartare sauce (see p. 63).

Blinis or Russian pancakes

To make these little pancakes successfully, you need a small frying pan of 10 cm (4 in) diameter. The batter is made with baker's yeast and needs 2½–3 hours to rise; but the cooking only take 3 minutes for each pancake. They can be kept, wrapped and sealed, in the refrigerator, and can even be frozen and reheated in a moderate oven. Blinis are served hot, accompanied by hot melted butter, cold cream and lemons, and with a garnish of smoked salmon, fish roes, caviar or other smoked or salted fish. You eat them by dipping in the melted butter, filling with the fish, coating with the cream and sprinkling with a little lemon juice.

For 24 blinis   500 ml (scant pint; 2¼ cups) milk
350 g (12½ oz; 2⅜ cups) flour
20 g (¾ oz) fresh yeast
3 eggs
½ teaspoon salt
butter

Heat the milk until warm (no more than 40°C/104°F). Take out half a glassful and dissolve the yeast in this. Put 75 g (2½ oz) flour into a bowl with the dissolved yeast and knead while adding enough milk to form a ball of soft dough. Cover the bowl and leave in a warm place until the dough has doubled in volume.

Put the rest of the flour into a bowl with the egg yolks, salt and yeast dough. Gradually mix in the rest of the warm milk until you have a smooth paste without lumps. Cover with a cloth and leave to rise in a warm place for 30 minutes.

Stir the paste, which should have the consistency of a slightly heavy pancake batter. Whisk the egg white to a firm snow and fold in. Grease your frying pan with a nut of butter, pour in 2 tablespoons batter and cook quickly, turning with a spatula when the surface is no longer liquid.

Mushroom pancakes

These are thin pancakes wrapped round a stuffing of button mushrooms, with ham, cream and Gruyère; they are then sprinkled with cream and grated cheese, and put in the oven to brown.

For 6
180 g (6¼ oz) cooked ham
250 g (8¾ oz) button mushrooms
1 lemon
100 g (3½ oz; ½ cup) butter
1 tablespoon flour
250 g (8¾ oz; 1 cup) fresh cream
80 g (2¾ oz) grated Gruyère cheese
salt, pepper, nutmeg
6–8 prepared pancakes (without sugar)

Finely chop the ham, and do the same with the mushrooms, rubbing them with lemon juice to keep them white. Lightly brown the ham without frying in 1 tablespoon butter. Then take out the ham, add another nut of butter and the mushrooms, and cook quickly over a brisk heat until their moisture has evaporated. Return the ham to the pan and, when all the ingredients are good and hot, sprinkle with the flour. Mix, moisten with 2 tablespoons cream and, when this is incorporated, add, by the spoonful, enough cream to give the consistency of a gruel, fairly heavy but not pasty. Then add 1 heaped tablespoon grated cheese, taste and season with salt, pepper and nutmeg.

Preheat the oven to 200°C/400°F/Mark 6. Put 1 tablespoon stuffing in each pancake, and fold loosely into a square parcel, bringing together the edges and then the two ends. Place in an ovenproof dish from which they can be served. season the rest of the cream with a little salt and pepper and pour it over. Sprinkle with the rest of the cheese, and dot with shavings of butter. Put in the hot oven and cook, basting occasionally, until the cream has thickened and the pancakes have turned a pale golden.

You can prepare the dish the day before, up to the stage when it is ready to go into the oven—the pancakes will not disintegrate in the cream.

Pan bagnat

Pan bagnat, the wonderful Mediterranean sandwich, is a picnic all on its own. There is scarcely any limit to its size, and it can range from a roll to a long French loaf; once wrapped in a sheet of foil or grease-proof paper, so that all the flavours are sealed in, you can slice it, still in the wrapping, into as many portions as you want.

For 1	1 white bread roll
individual	2 tablespoons olive oil
pan bagnat	1 small garlic clove (optional)
	½ sweet pepper
	1 tomato
	1 onion
	4–6 tinned anchovy fillets in oil
	6 small black olives
	4–5 radishes

Split the roll in two and dribble plenty of olive oil over both halves. With the garlic press, squeeze a little garlic over one half. Put the sweet pepper under the grill to skin it, and remove the seeds (those with more robust stomachs add it raw). Cut the tomato and onion into rounds, and slice the radishes.

Arrange the tomato, onion, sweet pepper, anchovy fillets, olives and radishes on one half of the roll, cover with the other half and wrap tightly in a sheet of foil. Although you will probably want to eat it straight away, leave it for a few minutes—it will taste even better.

Pissaladière

This speciality of Nice is basically an onion tart, but the pastry and onions are prepared in a special way, which makes it a great delicacy and an appetizer.

This recipe
is from
Mme Raibaut-
Dumas
For 6

THE PASTRY
250 g (8¾ oz; 1¾ cups) flour
15 g (½ oz) fresh yeast
a pinch of salt
2½ tablespoons olive oil
flan dish 24–26 cm (10 in) diameter

THE FILLING
1 kg (2 lb 4 oz) onions
3 tablespoons olive oil
100 g (3½ oz) small black olives
salt, pepper

Heap the flour on your worktop or board and make a well in the centre. Dissolve the yeast in 2 tablespoons warm water, and add to the flour with the salt and oil. Work together, first with your finger-tips, then with your hands. As soon as the dough is smooth and supple, form it into a ball without leaving it to rest. Place on a circular metal tart tin of 26 cm (10 in) diameter, greased with oil, and spread it out with your hands to an even thickness. Then leave to rest in the refrigerator for 30 minutes.

Slice the onions, don't chop them, and put in a large frying pan. Pour in water and the oil to come half way up their depth, and season with salt and pepper. Cook over a moderate heat until the water has evaporated, leaving only the oil, and the onions are soft and trans-parent but not melted to a purée. Leave to cool slightly.

Preheat the oven to 200°C/400°F/Mark 6. Spread the pastry with the onions, scatter the olives on top and put in the hot oven, just below the middle, to bake. Make sure that the pastry is well cooked, golden and crisp and serve warm.

Potato tart

This looks like a large, golden cake and is a comforting, yet delicately-flavoured, entrée, which is easy to make. It should be served a little hotter rather than warm, but not piping hot.

For 6–8   2×250 g (8 oz) packets frozen puff pastry
2 kg (4 lb 8 oz) potatoes
3 medium onions
1 yolk of egg
1 large bunch of herbs—chives, tarragon, parsley
175 g (6 oz; ⅝ cup) fresh cream
salt, pepper, nutmeg
flan dish 26–28 cm (10–11 in) diameter

Thaw the pastry overnight in the bottom of the refrigerator. Roll out the pastry from one packet very thinly—4–5 mm (¼ in) thick—and line the unbuttered flan dish, leaving an overlap of 3 cm (1 in) all round. Slice the potatoes into very thin rounds and chop the onions finely. Cover the pastry base with about a quarter of the potatoes in a shallow layer, season with salt and pepper, grate over a little nutmeg and sprinkle with 1 tablespoon onion. Repeat twice and finish with a layer of potatoes.

Preheat the oven to 200°C/400°F/Mark 6. Roll out the pastry from the second packet slightly thinner than the first. Trace a decorative diamond pattern on it with the point of a knife and, with the rolling pin, lift it on top of the tart tin as a lid. Trim the edges to the same overlap as the first pastry round, wet your fingers and join the edges, pressing them together and rolling them up like a scroll. Using a pastry brush, glaze the whole tart with the egg yolk beaten with a few drops of water. Make oblique cuts with the scissors every 3 cm (1 in) round the scroll and, with a knife, pierce 6 slits in the pastry close to the edge for the steam to escape.

Put the tart in the oven, on the first rung up from the bottom and, after 20 minutes, turn down the heat to 160°C/320°F/Mark 3. Bake for about 2 hours 30 minutes altogether, keeping an eye on the colour and, if necessary, covering with a sheet of absorbent paper for protection. Meanwhile, chop the herbs to give 4 tablespoons, with the parsley predominating, and mix with the cream plus a tiny pinch of salt. Leave at room temperature to draw out the flavours. When the tart is cooked, lift off the lid around the scroll and sprinkle the potatoes with the cream and herbs. Put back the lid and return the tart to the oven for 10 minutes, with the heat turned off or very low.

Snail quiche

Make this with frozen puff pastry and the small snails known as 'petits gris', which have rough, brownish shells, and give more flavour to this dish than the larger vineyard variety.

For 6   300 g (10½ oz) frozen puff pastry
butter, flour
½ tin of snails (preferably 'petits gris')
1 large leek
50 g (1¾ oz; ¼ cup) butter
1–2 shallots
1 clove of garlic (optional)
2 tablespoons chervil leaves
3 eggs
250 g (8¾ oz; 1 cup) fresh cream
salt, pepper, nutmeg
flan dish 24–26 cm (10 in) diameter

Thaw the frozen pastry overnight in the bottom of the refrigerator. Roll out without kneading and line the previously buttered and lightly floured flan dish. Turn the tin to shake off excess flour and leave in a cool place for 30 minutes.

Turn the snails into a colander, rinse them under cold water and drain thoroughly. Slice the white part of the leek and soften gently in half the butter. In a separate pan, soften the chopped shallots in the rest of the butter, and add the snails, cooking just long enough to draw out the flavours without stiffening them. Some people add a touch of garlic, squeezed through the garlic press.

Preheat the oven to 230°C/450°F/Mark 8. Prick the base of the pastry with a fork, spread with a layer of half the leeks, followed by the snails and shallots, season with salt and pepper and sprinkle with the chervil, and cover with the rest of the leeks. Beat the eggs with the cream, season with salt, pepper and nutmeg and ladle over the filling. Place in the oven, on the first rung from the bottom, and keep an eye on the colour of the filling and the progress of the cooking. Basically, the quiche is cooked when stiff as you carefully lift the edge, and will take 30–35 minutes. Serve 10 minutes after taking out of the oven, that is to say, between piping hot and warm.

Spinach tart

For 6

1×250 g (8 oz) packet frozen puff pastry
500 g (1 lb 2 oz) spinach (after trimming)
1 large bunch of chervil
60 g (2 oz; ¼ cup) butter
2 tablespoons flour
250 g (8¾ oz; 1 cup) pouring cream
4 eggs
salt, pepper, nutmeg, sugar
flan dish 24–26 cm (10 in) diameter

Thaw the pastry overnight in the bottom of the refrigerator. Pick over and thoroughly wash the spinach (or use frozen spinach). Add to 2 litres (3½ pints; 4½ US pints) boiling salted water, return to the boil and cook for 2 minutes. Remove from the heat, refresh the spinach in cold water, drain and pat dry. Then chop the spinach and squeeze it with your hands or in a cloth to get rid of all the moisture. Season with salt, pepper and nutmeg. Roughly chop the chervil leaves and mix with the spinach.

Melt the butter in a large saucepan, put in the flour and cook for 2 minutes while stirring. Pour in the cream, cook until thickened and season lightly with salt, pepper and nutmeg. Beat the eggs and, off the fire, combine them with the cream sauce. Set aside one third of this mixture, and mix the rest with the spinach. Taste and correct the seasoning as necessary, adding a small pinch of sugar if the spinach seems too bitter.

Preheat the oven to 200°C/400°F/Mark 6 for 15 minutes. Take the buttered and lightly floured flan dish, roll out the pastry very thinly— just 5 mm (¼ in) thick—and line the tin with it and prick the base with the point of a knife or a fork. Pour in the spinach filling, and cover with the reserved cream and egg sauce. Put in the oven, placing it a quarter of the way up from the bottom, and after 20 minutes reduce the heat to 180°C/350°F/Mark 4. Bake for about another 20 minutes, keeping an eye on the colour, and test to see if it is done by shaking the tin—the pastry should basically be crisp and detached from the tin. Turn off the oven and leave the tart to rest for 5–10 minutes with the door open. Serve warm rather than hot.

Tomato and basil tart

This is an original entrée. The type of mustard you choose is very important—I would recommend a classic mustard without additional flavourings, but it depends on individual taste, and experience may lead you to decide otherwise.

For 6

1×50 g (8 oz) roll of frozen puff pastry
butter, flour
1 tablespoon basil leaves
150 g (5¼ oz) Gruyère cheese
4 tomatoes
2 tablespoons pure yellow mustard
salt, pepper
flan dish 24–26 cm (10 in) diameter

Thaw the puff pastry overnight in the bottom of the refrigerator. Flour and lightly butter the flan dish. Roll out the pastry very thinly—3–4 mm (2 in) thick—and line the tin, without stretching it too much around the sides. Refrigerate while you make the filling.

Preheat the oven to 230°C/450°F/Mark 8. Roughly chop the basil and slice the cheese (don't grate it). Skin and de-seed the tomatoes, and cut into quarters, not rounds. Spread the base of the pastry case with the mustard, adding a little more if necessary, to obtain an even layer of about 4 mm (¼ in). Cover with the cheese, interspersed with the basil, and finish with the tomatoes. Season lightly with salt and pepper. The tomatoes give the effect of beautiful red fruits and, in cooking, the cheese will melt to fill the spaces in between, making the tart very attractive. Bake quickly, with the tin positioned just below the centre of the oven, and keep an eye on the progress and the colour of the pastry, which should be crisp when cooked. Serve warm.

Natural salad with herbs

An attractive, simple entrée to sharpen the appetite, rich in vitamins and mineral salts, and offering the balance of good nourishment.

For 6	250 g (8¾ oz) French beans
	1 cucumber
	½ cauliflower
	1 bunch of radishes
	1 bunch of watercress
	1 bunch of chervil
	2 branches of tarragon
	1 onion
	4 tablespoon olive oil
	1 tablespoon vinegar
	mustard, salt, pepper
	1 lettuce
	1 bowl of mayonnaise (see p.58)

Cook the French beans in boiling salted water so that they remain 'al dente', that is, still firm; refresh quickly in cold water and cut into pieces. Wash the cucumber but don't peel it, and slice into very thin rounds. Separate the cauliflower into small florets. Cut half the radishes into rounds, and shape the other half to look like open flowers. reserving these for garnish. Finely chop the watercress leaves together with the chervil and tarragon leaves and onion. Add to a vinaigrette, made with the oil, vinegar, a little mustard and salt and pepper. Put all the prepared ingredients in a bowl, mix together and leave in a cool place for 25–30 minutes to allow the flavours to blend.

Wash the lettuce. Cut the heart into thin ribbons, and mix with the rest of the salad, adding 2 good spoons of mayonnaise. Line the bottom of the serving dish with the large leaves of the lettuce, add the salad and garnish with the reserved radishes. Hand the rest of the mayonnaise round in a sauceboat.

White cabbage salad

This winter salad-starter has a very refreshing taste and is rich in vitamins, particularly the antiscorbutic vitamin C; it also provides sulphur, another element essential for the body at that time of year.

For 6   1 white cabbage
5–6 tablespoons olive oil flavoured with thyme
4–5 juniper berries (optional)
2 lemons
salt, pepper from the mill

Cut the cabbage into quarters. With a strong knife on a wooden board, slice into thin strips, discarding the large ribs. Wash and dry in a cloth. Arrange the cabbage in a salad bowl, and season with 1 scant teaspoon salt and a generous grinding of pepper. Sprinkle with 5–6 tablespoons oil, according to the size of the cabbage, add the crushed juniper berries and stir. Squeeze over the juice of 1 lemon, mix again, and leave to macerate for 1½–2 hours, stirring occasionally.

Just before serving, taste and correct the seasoning according to personal preference; the salad should be fairly highly flavoured. Add more lemon juice if necessary, but only at this stage.

Spinach salad

For 6   1 kg (2 lb 4 oz) young spinach
3 lemons
olive oil
salt, pepper from the mill

Pull off the spinach stalks, at the same time removing the large central rib of the leaves, wash in several changes of water, and drain. Bring to the boil plenty of salted water—at least 2 litres (3½ pints; 4½ US pints)—and cook the spinach in stages, adding a handful of the leaves, leaving for 1 minute, then removing with a skimmer and placing in a colander to drain. When all the spinach has been cooked in this way, drain thoroughly and refrigerate.

Serve the spinach in a dish decorated with a few thin slices of lemon, and accompanied by a flask of olive oil, halved lemons, a salt cellar and peppermill. Everyone seasons their share of the spinach to their own taste, or you can make up a vinaigrette in a sauceboat to pass around the table.

If you grow your own spinach, choose young, well-shaped leaves, prepare them as for a salad, arrange in a salad bowl and dress with a vinaigrette made with good quality olive oil.

Tabbouleh

Somewhere between a salad and an hors d'oeuvre, this is a sort of cold, raw semolina. It is made at least three hours in advance, using the semolina in its crude state, which then swells in the juice of the tomatoes and lemons and the oil. It is eaten as a starter, but also goes well with barbecued meat and cold dishes. In the Middle East, where it originated, tabbouleh is based on cracked wheat, but it can also be made with semolina which may be easier to obtain.

For 6

250 g (8¾) medium semolina or cracked wheat
12 small white onions
2 tablespoons finely chopped parsley
1 tablespoon chopped fresh mint, or crushed dried
    mint
750 g (1 lb 10½ oz) ripe tomatoes
6 tablespoons groundnut or olive oil
2 lemons
salt, pepper

Slice 8 of the small onions, skin the tomatoes and dice most of them, cutting a few into quarters. Reserve these quarters, the 4 onions and a small bunch of mint for the garnish. Put the semolina or cracked wheat into a dish with the sliced onions, the parsley and mint, the tomatoes together with their juice, the oil, salt and pepper, and the juice of the lemons. Mix thoroughly and leave in a cool place for at least 3 hours, stirring occasionally.

By the time you are ready to serve, the semolina or cracked wheat will have doubled in volume and there will be no liquid left in the bowl. Transfer the chilled tabbouleh to a salad bowl, garnish with the reserved tomatoes and onions, and place the mint in the middle.

Salade niçoise

Anchovies, olives from Nice—the smallest variety but so full of flavour—hard-boiled eggs, olive oil, sweet peppers, French beans, tomatoes . . . What a beautful sunny dish!

For 6–8   200 g (7 oz) salted anchovies, or 1 tin anchovy fillets in oil
4 potatoes
200 g (7 oz) French beans
1 lettuce or curly endive
1 head of celery
4 firm tomatoes
2 sweet peppers, red and green
100 g (3½) small black olives
2 hard-boiled eggs
1 medium tin tuna fish in oil
olive oil
wine vinegar
salt, pepper

If you are using salted anchovies, fillet them under the cold tap, pat dry and soak in olive oil. Boil the potatoes in their skins and, when cold, cut into rounds. Cook the French beans in boiling salted water, without a lid, so that they remain green and firm; drain and slice each into 2–3 pieces. Cut the lettuce or endive and the celery into fine strips, and the tomatoes into quarters. Remove the seeds from the sweet peppers and slice into very thin rounds. Cut the hard-boiled eggs into 2 or 4, and the tuna into chunks.

Starting with the potatoes, assemble the ingredients in layers in a salad bowl, following the order above. Add the anchovies and half the olives after the sweet peppers, and finish with the hard-boiled eggs, tuna and the rest of the olives. Make a vinaigrette with the olive oil, wine vinegar and salt and pepper, and pour over the salad. Mix when you serve it.

Péigord salad

This salad is madly extravagant, but so, *so* beautiful . . . and an excellent opening for a celebration meal.

For 6
2 artichokes
300 g (10½ oz) fine French beans
500 g (1 lb 2 oz) green asparagus
1 curly endive, or 200 g (7 oz) 'mesclun'* (mixed green saladings)
1 truffle
200 g (7 oz) foie gras
groundnut oil
sherry vinegar, or very dry sherry
salt, pepper

Remove the leaves and chokes from the artichokes to leave only the hearts (see p. 81), and dip them in lemon juice to prevent them blackening. Cook them in boiling salted water until a needle can be stuck in them, but no longer. Refresh in cold water and cut into quarters. Cook the French beans in plenty of salted water, without a lid. As soon as they are tender, but still with some bite, rinse them in cold water and drain. Prepare the asparagus (see p. 82) and cook in the same way as the beans, keeping slightly firm as well. Wash and trim the endive or 'mesclun'. Slice the truffle, without peeling it, into very thin rounds.

Divide the prepared ingredients between each dish, and don't overdo the quantities. Top each portion with 2 fine slivers of foie gras, and set aside in a cool place. Just before serving dress each salad with a vinaigrette, made with the oil, sherry vinegar or dry sherry (which is even more delicate), salt and pepper.

The hostess will certainly be heaped with praise!

*Mesclun is a speciality of Provence, usually including cress, lettuce, lamb's lettuce, dandelion leaves, endive, chicory, fennel, chervil, all sown close together and gathered young together.

Chicken salad

This kind of salad is much appreciated by everyone, whatever the season. It is somewhat lengthy to prepare, and must be nicely presented. But it makes a complete meal on its own.

For 6–8
1 small chicken weighing 900 g–1 kg (2 lb–2 lb 4 oz)
1 sachet powdered court-bouillon
100 g (3½ oz; ½ cup) rice
½ small tin sweetcorn
1 small head of celery
2–3 very firm tomatoes
2 apples (preferably Cox)
1 cup watercress leaves
1 endive or escarole
a few branches of tarragon
oil, vinegar
salt, pepper
1 onion
200 ml (⅓ pint; ⅞ cup) mayonnaise (see p. 58)
125 g (4¼ oz) black olives

Put the chicken into a large pan, sprinkle with the powdered court-bouillon, cover with cold water and bring to the boil. Simmer for 20–25 minutes, then allow to cool in the liquid, with the lid off. Remove the skin from the chicken, carve off all the meat and cut into thin slices.

Cook the rice in salted water, rinse in cold water and drain thoroughly. Drain the tinned sweetcorn. Cut the celery sticks into cubes of about 1 cm (½ in), and dice the tomatoes, skinned and de-seeded, and the apples smaller. Finely chop the watercress leaves (reserving a few bunches for the garnish) with the heart of the endive or escarole and the tarragon leaves. Mix all the prepared ingredients together. Make a good cupful of vinaigrette with the oil, vinegar, salt and pepper and the finely chopped onion; it should be strongly flavoured and not too diluted. Sprinkle over the salad and leave to macerate for 1 hour.

Line the salad bowl with the green outer leaves of the endive. Mix

2 tablespoons mayonnaise and the olives with the salad, and turn into the bowl. Trim with the reserved watercress, serve, and hand the rest of the mayonnaise round at the same time.

Danish egg cake

This is a huge omelette, and comes to the table straight from the frying pan or omelette dish. It is sliced like a cake, each portion containing a piece of smoked bacon, and is completely covered with chives, roughly cut with scissors. Served with a salad, this rustic dish makes a meal on its own.

For 6   10 eggs
6 square slabs of smoked bacon, 1 cm (½ in) thick
60 g (2 oz; ¼ cup) butter
1 large bunch of chives
salt, pepper

Beat the eggs together with 5 tablespoons water and season with salt and pepper. Cook the bacon slices in a frying pan until golden. Melt the butter in an omelette pan of 24 cm (10 in) diameter, pour in the beaten eggs and cook slowly, using a fork to distribute the mixture, and then tipping the pan from front to back so that the eggs are evenly cooked and the omelette is soft and melting throughout, but not liquid. Then add the hot bacon and cover with the chives, cut up with scissors.

In Denmark they wrap the handle of the pan in foil so that it can be passed round the table.

Dariole eggs

Darioles are small, cylindrical moulds which have given their name to an old-fashioned cake. They are still used in cookery, and especially in restaurants for decorative moulds of rice, fruit jelly or mousses. Dariole moulds made with eggs, cream and cheese, are a good starter—easy to prepare, delicious and different.

For 6   6 eggs
            60 g (2 oz) thick cream
            70 g (2½ oz) grated Gruyère cheese
            70 g (2½ oz; ¼–⅜ cup) butter
            oil
            salt, pepper
            6 rounds white bread

Beat the eggs with the cream and cheese, reserving 1 tablespoon of the latter, and season with salt and pepper. Take 6 dariole moulds, butter them and sprinkle with the rest of the cheese. Divide the mixture between the moulds, filling them only three-quarters full, and place in a wide pan containing enough boiling water to come half way up the sides of the moulds. Put the lid on the pan and poach steadily for about 20 minutes. When the mixture has risen to the top of the moulds and no longer yields to the touch, the darioles are cooked.

Meanwile, toast the bread and fry until golden in half butter and half oil. Take the darioles out of the water and unmould while still hot on to the toast. Serve with a tomato sauce (see p. 63), highly seasoned with fines herbes or basil.

Eggs with sorrel and chervil

These eggs are cooked and served in little cocotte dishes or ramekins. The recipe can be adapted using mushrooms, tomatoes or asparagus as the accompaniment; the chosen ingredient should be carefully prepared, delicately seasoned and cooked rapidly in butter.

For 6   500 g (1 lb 2 oz) sorrel
            1 bunch of chervil
            125 g (4¼ oz; ½ cup) butter
            6 eggs
            200 g (7 oz; ¾ cup) cream
            salt, pepper, nutmeg

Remove the stalks and large ribs from the sorrel leaves, and cut into thin strips. Pick off the leaves of the chervil, and reserve half for the garnish. Over a brisk heat, quickly soften the sorrel and half the chervil in a third of the butter, stirring with a wooden spoon. When all is reduced to a cream, take off the heat, season with salt and pepper, and, if you like, grate in a little nutmeg. Divide the mixture between 6 individual cocotte dishes.

Break an egg into each dish. Season the cream lightly with salt and pepper, and pour over so that the yolks just show through. Dot with a shaving of butter. Place the dishes on an asbestos sheet over a high heat and when the cream comes to the boil remove immediately. Sprinkle the rest of the chervil, leave to rest for 2–3 minutes, then serve.

Gougère

This ring of cheese-flavoured choux pastry, baked in the oven, is eaten as a hot starter. Since it is put into the oven on a baking sheet, there is no restriction to its size.

For 6   250 ml (scant ½ pint; 1⅛ cups) water
100 g (3½ oz; ½ cup) butter
150 g (5¼ oz; 1 cup) flour
4 eggs, and 1 extra for glazing
150 g (5¼ oz) Emmenthal cheese
salt, pepper

Make up the choux paste following the recipe on p. 235, and season lightly with salt and pepper. Slice the cheese into small, thin strips (don't grate it, which would make the pastry heavy), and incorporate.

Preheat the oven to 180°C/350°F/Mark 4. Lightly grease and flour a baking sheet, and trace out a circle. Using a tablespoon or, better, a forcing bag fitted with a size 12 nozzle, arrange the paste in a circle, with each dollop the size of an egg and spaced 2 cm (1 in) apart. Brush with the beaten egg, and put in the medium oven, leaving the door half open for the first 6–7 minutes to allow the steam to escape, and then closing it. Bake for 25 minutes altogether. Turn off the oven, open the door and wait for 4–5 minutes before taking out the gougère, so that it doesn't collapse.

Omelette in a dish

Although it is difficult to make omelettes with more than 6 eggs, this one will take as many as the dish allows. It is an omelette for improvised dinners, and can be made with all the classic ingredients like mushrooms, bacon or fines herbes. It is one of the finest.

For 6
700 g (1 lb 9 oz) potatoes
125 g (4¼ oz; ½ cup) butter
1–2 tablespoons oil
1 clove of garlic
10–12 eggs
salt, pepper

Cook the potatoes in their skins and allow to cool. Slice into rounds, and sauté in a frying pan in a mixture of half butter, half oil, until golden. At the last minute, add the crushed garlic. Turn into a long ovenproof dish, season with salt and pepper, stir and smooth the surface. The oven should be preheated to the highest temperature, and a baking sheet ready on the lowest rung, for 15 minutes before the dish is to go in.

Beat the eggs, season lightly with salt and pepper, and pour over the potatoes. Put in the oven and, as soon as the surface of the omelette sets, dot with a few nuts of butter and turn down the heat or leave the oven door half open. The omelette should be firm, but must not bubble. Leave to cook for 15–20 minutes, or until the top is a beautiful pale golden and is coming away from the edges of the dish. Turn the oven off, leave with the door open for 3–4 minutes, then serve the omelette.

Pipérade

This is the omelette of the Basque country, garnished with sweet pepper, tomatoes, onions and Bayonne ham. It is a delicious entrée or a light supper dish.

For 6
4 sweet peppers, red or green
1 kg (2 lb 4 oz) tomatoes
1 onion
1 clove of garlic

olive oil
6 thin slices Bayonne ham
6 eggs
salt, pepper

Put the sweet peppers under the grill to skin them, remove the seeds and cut into chunks. Skin and de-seed the tomatoes, and chop roughly. Slice the onion. Heat 2 tablespoons olive oil in a large frying pan and soften the onion without letting it brown. Add the sweet peppers and, when they are almost cooked, the tomato flesh and crushed garlic. Season with salt and pepper and cook gently until reduced to a cream.

Meanwhile, fry the ham in a separate pan, remove and keep hot. Deglaze the pan with a spoonful or two of the vegetable cream and pour back into the main frying pan. Beat the eggs and, off the heat, mix into the vegetables. Cook gently, stirring all the time to prevent the mixture becoming too lumpy. As soon as it is smooth and creamy, with no liquid, transfer to the serving dish and garnish with the fried ham.

Lasagne bolognese

Lasagne is a type of pasta in wide flat strips. It should be cooked with care, so as not to break the strips, which are built up in layers on top of each other with the stuffing in between. This dish should be prepared in two stages: it can be refrigerated for up to 48 hours before the final cooking, with the result that it will be a gratin dish of great delicacy. It is equally good as the entrée on a special occasion, or as the main course following an hors d'oeuvre of crudités.

For 6
1 × 500 g (1 lb 2 oz) packet of lasagne
2 tablespoons oil
50 g (1¾ oz; ¼ cup) butter
500 ml (scant pint; 2¼ cups) concentrated bolognese sauce (p. 55)
30 g (1 oz) grated Parmesan cheese
150 g (5¼ oz) Mozzarella cheese
250 g (8¾ oz; 1 cup) thick cream
50 g (1¾ oz) grated Gruyère cheese
salt, pepper

Bring to the boil in a large pan 5 litres (8¾ pints; 11¼ US pints) water with the oil and 1 tablespoon salt. Add the lasagne strips one at a time, cooking them in several batches to prevent them sticking together. Remove from the pan when they are tender but still resistant, and drain. Spread out on a damp cloth, stretching the strips without tearing, and leave to cool.

Take a rectangular dish 25 cm long and 5 cm deep (10 in and 2 in), and butter it generously. Arrange a quarter of the lasagne in the bottom and cover with a third of the bolognese sauce. Sprinkle with 1 tablespoon Parmesan and a third of the Mozzarella, cut into strips, and dot with a few shavings of butter. Repeat twice more, finish with a layer of lasagne and tap the side of the dish to settle the ingredients. Cover with a sheet of foil and leave to rest for 12 hours in the refrigerator.

Preheat the oven to 180°C/350°F/Mark 4. Unmould the lasagne onto a board and divide into square slabs, one for each person. Arrange them without touching in an ovenproof serving dish. Season the cream with salt and pepper, and pour over, and spread the grated Gruyère on top. Bake in the oven for 40 minutes, basting from time to time, until the lasagne is heated right through and the surface is golden. It is better to cook slowly than too fast.

Alternatively, you can cook the lasagne whole in its dish, immediately after assembling it in layers with the sauce and cheese; cover it with the cream and Gruyère and a few nuts of butter. The result will be less subtle, but delicious nevertheless.

Pasta with basil

To make this savoury dish, you should choose hollow tubes of pasta or rigatoni so that the basil paste will penetrate and make a delicious stuffing.

For 6	15–20 large basil leaves
	3 cloves of garlic
	100 g (3½ oz) grated Gruyère cheese
	2½ tablespoons olive oil
	500 g (1 lb 2 oz) pasta, preferably rigatoni
	30 g (1 oz; ⅛ cup) butter
	salt, pepper

Start by making the basil paste. Crush the garlic and basil leaves to a cream in a mortar. Then add the cheese by the spoonful, moistening with a little of the olive oil, to obtain a soft but not runny paste.

Bring to the boil 3 litres (5¼ pints; 6½ US pints) salted water in a large pan and add 1 tablespoon oil to prevent the pasta sticking together. Throw in the pasta, bring back to the boil and then cook for about 15–18 minutes. Taste to check when done. Turn into a colander to drain, and return to the dried and still hot pan. Season lightly with pepper and add the basil paste. Mix in thoroughly and transfer to the heated serving dish with a nut of butter at the bottom. Serve at once.

Vegetables

Catalan-style aubergines (egg plant)

A vegetable dish to serve on its own, or with grilled or roast meat. Aubergines cooked in this way are pleasing both to the eye and to the palate.

For 6　　　4 aubergines (egg plant)
　　　　　　frying oil
　　　　　　olive oil
　　　　　　3 tomatoes
　　　　　　2 cloves of garlic
　　　　　　3 tablespoons chopped parsley
　　　　　　1 tablespoon breadcrumbs
　　　　　　salt, pepper

　Choose long, firm aubergines. Cut them lengthwise into slices about 1 cm (½ in) thick, but without cutting right through at the base, and open them out like a fan. Sprinkle each slice with salt and leave for 20–30 minutes for the juices to drain off (especially late in the season when they can be a little bitter).

　Rinse and pat dry the aubergines. Heat the frying oil in a frying pan and add the aubergines one at a time, still spread out, just to colour them to a golden brown without trying to cook them. Drain and arrange in a long ovenproof dish. Season the slices with pepper and gloss with a few spoonfuls of olive oil.

　Preheat the oven to 200°C/400°F/Mark 6. Skin and de-seed the tomatoes and cut in half. Chop the garlic and parsley together, mix with the breadcrumbs, season with salt and pepper and moisten with a few drops of olive oil. Sprinkle most of this mixture over the tomato halves, reserving some for the garnish, and arrange the tomatoes with the aubergines. Bake in the oven for 25–30 minutes and, a few minutes before serving, sprinkle the rest of the garlic and parsley mixture over the whole dish.

Stuffed aubergines (egg plant)

In this recipe the aubergines are baked after a preliminary frying; they are opened out like a fan, each slice interleaved with cheese, tomato and sweet pepper, and the whole flavoured with onion, garlic and parsley.

For 6
3 medium aubergines (egg plant)
2 sweet peppers
4 large onions
olive oil
frying oil
3 tomatoes
200 g (7 oz) fresh, uncured cheese, curd cheese, or
   Mozzarella
1 large bunch of parsley
3 cloves of garlic
salt, pepper

Wash the aubergines without peeling them, and cut lengthwise into slices without cutting right through to the base. Sprinkle with salt and leave for 30 minutes for the juices to drain out. Peel the sweet peppers, remove the seeds and slice into strips. Chop the onions, and soften them without colouring in the olive oil in a frying pan. Set aside and put in the sweet peppers to soften for a few minutes in the same pan. Cut the tomatoes into rounds, and slice the cheese. Rinse and dry the aubergines. In the frying oil, fry each one in turn to soften, with the slices still opened out. Leave to drain on kitchen paper, and pat dry.

Preheat the oven to 230°C/450°F/Mark 8. Cover the bottom of an ovenproof dish with the onions, and arrange the aubergines on top in a rosette shape, with a round of tomato, a slice of cheese and a few strips of sweet pepper between each slice. Season with a little salt and with pepper, and sprinkle with 1–2 tablespoons olive oil. Chop the parsley and garlic together and strew generously over the surface. Bake in the oven for about 35 minutes, covering with a sheet of foil when heated through. Don't let the parsley burn.

Scarlet cabbage

This is the familiar red cabbage, cooked in the oven virtually as it is. It goes with all rich and fatty roasts, such as pork, goose and duck.

For 6
2–3 red cabbages
150 ml (¼ pint; ⅝ cup) wine or cider vinegar
nutmeg, or 6 juniper berries
300 g (10½ oz) redcurrant jelly
butter
salt, pepper

Cut the red cabbages into quarters, wash them without breaking them up, drain and dry. Slice into fine strips on a board, discarding the large ribs. Transfer to a colander or strainer and slowly pour through 3 litres (5¼ pints; 6½ US pints) boiling salted water; the cabbage will turn purple. Drain thoroughly and turn into a bowl. Sprinkle with the vinegar, stirring so that all the strips are moistened, and the cabbage will now become bright red.

Preheat the oven to 180°C/350°F/Mark 4. Take an ovenproof earthenware or china dish and transfer the cabbage to it by hand, shaking off the vinegar. Season with salt and pepper, and the nutmeg or crushed juniper berries. Cover with the redcurrant jelly, stir, and dot with butter. Put in the moderate oven and stir occasionally, making sure that the surface does not brown. After 25–30 minutes, the cabbage will be cooked, but will still be crisp and a brilliant red colour. If you can't serve it immediately, cover it with a sheet of foil. For goose, accompany the red cabbage with apples sautéed in butter or a purée of celeriac.

Glazed carrots

This dish is made with small spring carrots, which are sold with their green tops.

For 6
2 bunches of small carrots weighing about 1.25 kg (2 lb 12¾ oz) altogether
60 g (2 oz; ¼ cup) butter
salt, pepper, sugar, parsley

Clean the carrots with a brush, but don't scrape them, and wipe. Take a wide saucepan, perhaps a deep frying or sauté pan, put in the carrots with enough water to cover, add the butter and season sparingly with salt and pepper. Cook over a moderate heat, without a lid.

When all the water has evaporated and the carrots are cooked, the butter will remain. Sprinkle with 1 heaped tablespoon caster sugar and sauté the carrots, shaking the pan; they will soon become glistening, as if varnished. Serve sprinkled with a little chopped parsley.

Braised celery

Celery, the improved form of a vigorous wild plant which sometimes appears naturally in gardens, is a vegetable of great delicacy. It is the choicest accompaniment for roast white meats, and lends itself to all cooking methods from braising to gratin, always after a preliminary blanching. Its virtues, in the canon of culinary herbs, are by no means negligible: celery is a stimulant and diuretic, and rich in vitamins A and C; and, finely chopped in a sauce, it gives a piquant flavour to a mixed salad.

For 6   4–6 heads of celery
100 g (3½ oz; ½ cup) butter
6 tablespoons chicken or beef consommé
salt, pepper

Trim the celery to a length of about 15 cm (6 in), which is the tenderest part, and discard the large or damaged stalks and the roots. Wash thoroughly, shaking in the water to dislodge any grit. Put in a pan of boiling salted water and, when it has come back to the boil, cook for 12–15 minutes. Drain and cut the heads of celery in half lengthwise.

Melt all the butter in a heavy metal pan, preferably oval. Add the celery, overlapping but as far as possible in a single layer, and moisten with the consommé. Cover the pan and braise over a gentle heat. Half way through the cooking, taste the juices and season accordingly with salt and pepper. The celery is cooked when the point of a knife will slip in easily. At that moment, turn up the heat to reduce the sauce until there is nothing left but butter, and serve. If the pieces seem too large, slice the celery with a very sharp knife in the serving dish, without separating the heads.

Cooked in this way, celery can be turned into a gratin dish by covering with a cheese-flavoured béchamel sauce, or a thick tomato sauce, or simply topped with grated Gruyère cheese mixed with a spoonful of breadcrumbs and browned in the oven.

Stewed chicory with cream

This is almost a purée of chicory, which is cut into matchstick or julienne strips. It doubles as a vegetable bed for the dishes which it accompanies and as a sauce, and goes very well with veal escalopes or cutlets, scallops, steamed fish like sea bass or turbot, and fillets of sole or John Dory.

For 6   6 medium heads of chicory
            1 tablespoon groundnut oil
            60 g (2 oz; ¼ cup) butter
            500 ml (scant pint; 2¼ cups) pouring cream
            salt, pepper, caster sugar

Allow 1 head of chicory per person. Do not soak or wash them, but simply remove any wilted outer leaves, cut across into 2–3, and take out the bitter core of the heart from the pieces nearest the root. Divide each piece in half lengthwise and place on a board. With a very sharp knife, slice lengthwise into thin julienne or matchstick strips (be careful of your nails!). At this stage, if you are worried that there might be some grit left, put in a colander and swirl under the cold tap, then drain and dry in a cloth.

Melt the oil and butter in a wide, heavy, frying or sauté pan, add the chicory and cook for about 10 minutes over a moderate heat, stirring with a wooden spoon, until the pieces become transparent but are still firm. Season with salt and pepper and 1 tablespoon sugar, and stir to mix. Turn up the heat and cook until the chicory is a deep golden colour, but not brown. Then pour in the cream and bring gently to the boil, so that it thickens and the chicory finishes cooking; it should remain slightly firm, and must not disintegrate. This is a dish which can be reheated, and the same proportions can be used for 8 heads of chicory.

Sautéed cucumber

For many people, cooked cucumber is a novelty and, from habit, we usually eat it raw in salads. Here it is treated like a vegetable, and served as an accompaniment to fish or white meat—it is a pleasant change from boiled potatoes or rice.

For 6   3 cucumbers
              60 g (2 oz; ¼ cup) butter
              2 tablespoons chopped green herbs (parsley, chervil, chives or tarragon), or a pinch of thyme
              a little garlic (optional)
              salt, pepper

Peel the cucumbers with a vegetable knife and slice them lengthwise into four. Remove the seeds if it is late in the season, then cut into dice. Bring 2 litres (3½ pints; 4½ US pints) salted water to the boil, add the cucumber, bring back to the boil and cook for 15 minutes. Test to see if it is done—it should be still firm, but not crisp. Turn into a colander and drain thoroughly.

Melt the butter in a large frying or sauté pan and put in the cucumber. Over a brisk heat, rapidly drive off the excess moisture, stirring all the time, then lower the heat and cook for 20–30 minutes, depending on the size of the pan (it is better if the cucumber is in a thin layer). Stir occasionally. Add the thyme, if you are using it, 10 minutes before the end, and perhaps a touch of garlic. Alternatively, sprinkle with the chosen herbs just before serving, and at that stage season with salt and pepper.

Curly endive loaf

Served with a tomato sauce enriched with ham, this is a complete meal; but it can also accompany roast or braised meat. It is equally good hot or cold, and a sandwich made with endive loaf, and perhaps some ham between it and the bread, is a good standby for a journey or a picnic.

For a 1 litre	4–6 heads of curly endive, according to size
(1³⁄₄ pints;	80 g (2³⁄₄ oz; ³⁄₈ cup) butter
4¹⁄₂ cups)	2 level tablespoons cream
charlotte	200 g (7 oz; ³⁄₄ cup) cream
mould	4 eggs
	salt, pepper, nutmeg
	fresh tomato sauce (see p. 63)
	125 g (4¹⁄₄ oz) cooked ham

Pick over the endive, discarding any wilted leaves but keeping all the green ones. Wash carefully. Add to 3 litres (5¼ pints; 6½ US pints) boiling salted water, return to the boil and cook, uncovered, for 12–15 minutes. Drain immediately and squeeze in bundles with your hands to remove all moisture. Then chop roughly on a board.

Preheat the oven to 180°C/350°F/Mark 4. Make a thick béchamel sauce (see p. 52) with 2 tablespoons of the butter, the flour and cream. Mix in the endive and add the beaten eggs. Taste, correct the seasoning which should be quite strong, and add a pinch of grated nutmeg. Generously butter the mould and fill with the mixture, tapping the mould on the table as you do so to prevent any air pockets. Place in 4–5 cm (2 in) water in a bain-marie, put in the oven and cook for 1 hour. Make sure that the water in the bain-marie does not boil, and that the surface of the loaf does not brown—it should just be a pale golden. To see if the loaf is cooked, insert the blade of a knife right down to the bottom, and it should come out clean. When it is ready, open the oven door and leave for 8–10 minutes before unmoulding onto the serving dish. Surround with a ribbon of hot tomato sauce, highly seasoned and with the finely chopped or diced ham mixed in.

Braised fennel

This aniseed-flavoured bulb is, like celery, one of those useful vegetables which is available before the arrival of spring vegetables. Try it, instead of boiled potatoes, with fish. When buying fennel, choose small bulbs, as they have a more delicate taste. And don't throw away the small, feathery leaves: cut with scissors, rather than chopped, they can be used to garnish a potato or green salad, as well as fried escalopes of turkey or veal.

For 6   8 small fennel bulbs
               2 tablespoons flour, or 1 large hunk of stale white
                 bread
               70 g (2½ oz; ¼–⅜ cup) butter, or 2 tablespoons goose
                 fat
               salt, pepper

Trim the fennel bulbs by removing the two or three outer leaves, shortening the stalks a little and cutting off the green shoots. Bring to the boil 3 litres (5¼ pints; 6½ US pints) salted water, with the addition of the flour mixed with a little cold water or the bread—this is to keep the fennel white. Put in the bulbs and cook until they can be pierced with a trussing needle, while remaining slightly resistant. Refresh in cold water and drain. Cut into halves or quarters, according to size, and pat dry.

Heat the butter or goose fat in a heavy metal pan or sauté pan, which will hold the fennel in no more than two layers. Add the fennel and cook without colouring over a moderate heat. When all the liquid has evaporated, season lightly with pepper, cover the pan and finish cooking over a very low heat. Serve the fennel as it is, or sprinkled with chopped fines herbes.

Sautéed mushrooms

For this dish, white cultivated or button mushrooms are used, simply cooked in butter and sprinkled with parsley. They are served as a vegetable rather than a garnish, and go with grilled steak, veal or pork, on their own or with a few fried potatoes.

For 6   1 kg (2 lb 4 oz) mushrooms
               2 lemons
               100 g (3½ oz; ½ cup) butter
               2 tablespoons chopped parsley
               salt, pepper

Choose very white, small button mushrooms with the caps still closed. Cut off the earthy end of the stalks and wash very quickly in water acidulated with the juice of 1 lemon. Drain and pat dry. Do not slice them, but cut in half—or in quarters if they are rather larger.

Without delay, put the mushrooms in a large frying pan with a nut of the butter and the juice of the other lemon, and cook until they have released their moisture, stirring occasionally. When they are swimming in liquid, pour off most of it and add the rest of the butter. Sauté the mushrooms until only the butter remains. Season with salt and pepper, and serve as soon as possible, sprinkled with the finely chopped parsley.

Fried parsley

The curly variety of parsley is used for frying, and you should choose pieces with long stalks. Wash and dry very thoroughly, or else the hot oil will splutter, and tie into bunches. Heat the frying oil until very hot, on the point of smoking, and plunge in the parsley, holding the stalks with a gloved hand. In a few seconds, it will be shrivelled but still green—don't let it turn brown. Take out carefully and place on absorbent kitchen paper. Season lightly with salt and cut off the stalks close to the cooked part. The parsley will become crisp as it cools. Only fry one bunch at a time, but serve a whole lot together in a dish—it cannot fail to be a success.

French-style peas

Fresh garden peas have such a fleeting season that they deserve this special treatment, which preserves all their delicate flavour. It's a taste you can't recapture at any other time of the year, either with tinned or frozen peas, although both have their virtues.

For 4
2 kg (4 lb 8 oz) small garden peas in their pods, giving about 1 kg (2 lb 4 oz) shelled peas
1 green lettuce
1 small bouquet garni of parsley, bayleaf and thyme
10–12 small, white, new onions
100 g (3½ oz; ½ cup) butter
1 sugar lump
salt, pepper

Shell the peas just before required, so that they will be at the peak of freshness. Remove the large outer leaves from the lettuce (they can be used in a salad), keeping only the heart, which should be about the size of a fist. Make a tiny bouquet garni with a sprig of parsley including the stalk, half a bayleaf and a small branch of thyme, all firmly tied together. Peel the onions, leaving on a little of the green tops—1 cm (½in)—and blanch in boiling salted water for 5 minutes. Put the peas and onions into a thick-bottomed pan such as an enamelled cast-iron casserole, make room for the lettuce heart in the middle and bury the bouquet garni in the peas. Add the sugar lump, season with salt and pepper, pour on half a glass of cold water, dot with half the butter and cover the pan. Cook over a fairly high heat, and do not lift the lid for 20 minutes. As soon as the peas are tender, remove the pan from the heat and discard the bouquet garni. Add the rest of the butter in pieces, shaking the pan so that it melts and mingles to form a velvety sauce. Turn into the serving dish with the lettuce heart in the centre.

Gratin dauphinois

This is the most straightforward and delicate of all potato gratin dishes, and basically includes just cream and milk. All its subtlety ts in the cooking, and on the total thickness of the layer of potatoes, which should not exceed 5 cm (2 in).

For 6   1 clove of garlic
30 g (1 oz; ⅛ cup) butter
1.5 kg (3 lb 6 oz) potatoes
350 ml (generous ½ pint; 1¼ cups) boiled milk
750 ml (1¼ pints; 3¼ cups) thick cream
salt, pepper, nutmeg.

Whatever the shape of the gratin dish, it is important that it should be of earthenware, china or glass, and that the sides should be 5 cm (2 in) deep, which restricts the thickness of the gratin. Begin by rubbing the base and sides of the dish with the garlic, let it dry and then butter liberally. Wash and peel the potatoes. Slice into rounds as thinly as possible and arrange in the dish.

Preheat the oven to 200°C/400°F/Mark 6. Heat the cream with the milk to boiling, season with salt, pepper and nutmeg, and taste—it should not be bland. Pour over the potatoes so that they are just covered, but no more, and put in the oven. Keep an eye on the dish for the first part of the cooking, as the milk might overflow, and if necessary, turn down the heat to 180°C/350°F/Mark 4. Then, before browning the top, cover with a sheet of foil, shiny side down. The gratin will need more than 1 hour of cooking, and at the end there should be no liquid left; but don't overcook, or else the cream will turn to oil. Once cooked, heat the grill, remove the foil and brown the surface under the grill.

Sarlat-style potatoes

These potatoes, usually sliced into rounds, are sautéed in goose fat, with a sliver of fresh truffle for special occasions. In the Périgord they accompany preserved goose or duck, roasts and grilled meats, like duck steak; and they are often served on their own with a walnut oil salad.

For 6 1.5 kg (3 lb 6 oz) potatoes
4 tablespoons goose fat
1 clove of garlic (optional)
1 truffle (optional)
salt, pepper

Slice the potatoes into rounds and plunge into 3 litres (5¼ pints; 6½ US pints) boiling water to get rid of the starch. Drain and pat dry. Heat the goose fat in a large frying pan with the crushed clove of garlic. Remove the garlic and add the potatoes, stirring without breaking them. If your frying pan is not large enough to hold the potatoes in a layer 4–5 cm (2 in) thick, use two pans. As soon as they begin to colour, season with salt and pepper, flatten into a cake and let them become crisp, without stirring. When they are a nice golden, turn them over, using a plate, to colour the other side.

A few minutes before serving, peel the truffle, chop the peelings and scatter over the potatoes. Slice the truffle thinly and distribute on top, sprinkling with a good spoonful of the goose fat. Cover the pan for 2–3 minutes to allow the flavours to develop, then slide the potato cake onto the serving dish.

Spinach in butter

In this dish, the spinach is cooked and served whole, not puréed or chopped, although the cooking method is a preliminary to all preparations in which it is chopped. Spinach goes particularly well with roast or grilled veal, pork or chicken. It is also rich in mineral salts, especially iron, and vitamins, and the pre-cooking in salted water, which only lasts a few minutes, does not rob it of these essentials.

For 6   2 kg (4 lb 8 oz) very fresh spinach
                 100 g (3½ oz; ½ cup) butter
                 salt, pepper, nutmeg

Pick over and trim the spinach, pulling out the stalks as far as the middle of the leaves. Wash carefully. Pre-cook the spinach in two or three batches: bring to the boil 3 litres (5¼ pints; 6½ US pints) salted water in a large saucepan; put in some of the spinach, return to the boil, cook for just 2–3 minutes and drain in a colander. Repeat until all the spinach is cooked, then press it in bundles between your hands to squeeze out the moisture.

Melt the butter in a frying pan and immediately add the spinach. Finish cooking over a very moderate heat, so that the butter does not brown. Taste and season with salt and pepper and a pinch of grated nutmeg. Garnish, if you like, with a few flaked almonds just before serving.

Provençal tomatoes

These tomatoes are cut in half, de-seeded, baked, and sprinkled with chopped garlic and parsley. They are both a garnish for grilled meats, and a delicious vegetable.

For 6   6 round, very red, firm tomatoes
                 2 teaspoons thyme leaves
                 1 teaspoon rosemary leaves
                 3 tablespoons olive oil
                 4 cloves of garlic
                 3 tablespoons parsley
                 2 tablespoons breadcrumbs
                 salt, pepper

Preheat the oven to 200°C/400°F/Mark 6. Wash and wipe the tomatoes, and cut them across into two equal halves. Arrange them in an ovenproof dish or baking tin with the cut side upwards. Season with salt and pepper, sprinkle with a pinch of mixed thyme and rosemary, and with a little olive oil—not too much. Put in the oven and bake for 15–20 minutes.

Meanwhile, chop the garlic and parsley very finely, add the bread-crumbs and mix well together. When the tomatoes are cooked, not collapsed but on the point of colouring, take them out of the oven. Spread each half with a good teaspoonful of the garlic mixture, and put under the grill for 5 minutes to brown. These tomatoes are usually served hot, but they are also very good cold.

Glazed turnips

The best turnips for this dish are the small, round ones, the first crop in spring. But if these are not available you can use large turnips, trimming each one to the size of an olive; the smaller the vegetables, the easier it is to glaze them.

For 4   2–3 bunches of small turnips, according to size, or
                 about 1 kg (2 lb 4 oz)
             100 (3½ oz; ½ cup) butter
             salt, pepper, caster sugar

Wash and peel the turnips. Put in a heavy metal pan or thick sauté pan, so that they will fit in 1 or 2 layers, no more. Pour in cold water to come half way up, add the butter, 1 level tablespoon sugar, and salt, put the lid on and bring to the boil. Then lower the heat and simmer gently, shaking the pan occasionally so that all the turnips are evenly cooked. Keep an eye on them and, when they can be pierced with the point of a knife, take the lid off the pan and continue to cook until all the water has evaporated and the turnips have turned crisp and golden in the butter.

Purée of three vegetables

This goes with venison, roast and grilled pork, braised sweetbreads and brains, roast duck and goose. All purées of watery vegetables, like celeriac, carrots, onions, turnips, Jerusalem artichokes, need to be thickened or given body by something else. You can choose between a thick béchamel sauce, or puréed potato. To me, the latter is preferable for several reasons: you can cook the potatoes in the same water and pan as the other vegetables, purée them with the same instrument, and they give a less pasty result.

For 6	3 medium celeriac
	1 lemon
	2 heaped tablespoons flour, or 1 fairly large piece of stale white bread
	80 g (2¾ oz; ⅜ cup) butter
	3 potatoes
	300 g (10½ oz) sorrel leaves
	125 g (4¼ oz; ½ cup) cream
	salt, pepper, nutmeg

Peel the celeriac and cut into pieces, rubbing with lemon juice to keep them white. Bring to the boil 3 litres (5¼ pints; 6½ US pints) salted water; remove from heat and add the flour, mixed with a little cold water, or the bread. Return to the boil, stirring all the time. Put in the celeriac, and half cover the pan, as it can boil over in the same way as milk. Boil gently until the celeriac can be pierced easily with a fork, and drain, reserving the water. Purée, using the fine blade of the vegetable mill; add half the butter and keep hot.

Peel the potatoes and cut into large chunks. Cook in the same water and pan as the celeriac, then drain thoroughly and purée in the same way. Gradually incorporate with the celeriac to give the right consistency; there is no need to use up all the potato purée, just enough to thicken without increasing the volume.

Pick over, trim and wash the sorrel, and cut into fine strips. Reserving one fifth for garnish, soften the rest in the remaining butter. As soon as the water has evaporated and the sorrel is reduced to a cream, add it to the purée. Mix thoroughly with a whisk, and season with pepper and, if you like, nutmeg. To serve, reheat the purée while whisking, add one or two spoonfuls of cream for perfect smoothness, and trim with the reserved, uncooked sorrel.

Ratatouille bohémienne

For 6	1 kg (2 lb 4 oz) aubergines (egg plant)
	1 kg (2 lb 4 oz) tomatoes
	500 g (1 lb 2 oz) onions
	1 tablespoon olive oil
	3 cloves of garlic
	8 tinned anchovy fillets in oil

1 tablespoon flour
½ tablespoon milk
2 tablespoons parsley
3 tablespoons white breadcrumbs
salt, pepper

Peel the aubergines, dice them and put in a colander with 2 spoonfuls salt. Stir and leave for 30 minutes for the juices to run. Skin and de-seed the tomatoes and cut into pieces. Slice the onions. Heat the milk to boiling and allow to cool.

Heat half the oil in an enamelled cast-iron casserole, and soften the onions without colouring. As soon as they are soft and transparent, add the aubergines, rinsed in cold water and dried. Brown lightly for 5 minutes, then put in the tomatoes and a whole clove of garlic, adding more oil if necessary. Cook gently, uncovered, stirring often. Pound the anchovies with their oil in a mortar, mixing with the flour and milk to obtain a smooth sauce. Add to the ratatouille when it is cooked and season with pepper. Taste and correct the seasoning, then turn into an ovenproof serving dish.

Preheat the oven to 230°C/450°F/Mark 8. Chop the rest of the garlic with the parsley, mix with the breadcrumbs and sprinkle over the surface of the dish. Place in the oven to reheat quickly and brown the top.

This ratatouille can also be served cold, as an hors d'oeuvre, with the addition of a few drops of vinegar or lemon juice.

Ratatouille niçoise

There are many different ways of making this celebrated ratatouille, and its certainly the olive oil which gives a true ratatouille its southern character. It is equally good hot or cold, but the ingredients must be well prepared for it to reach the height of flavour, and it's not a dish that can be improvised.

For 6–8   6 aubergines (egg plant)
                   6 courgettes (squash)
                   6 tomatoes
                   2 sweet peppers (optional)
                   10–12 small onions weighing 300 g (10½ oz)
                      altogether
                   500 ml (scant pint; 2¼ cups) olive oil
                   1 bouquet garni
                   1 small sprig of oregano
                   3 cloves of garlic
                   salt, pepper

Carefully wash all the vegetables. With a vegetable knife, peel the aubergines and courgettes in alternate stripes about 1.5 cm (½ in) wide, and cut into cubes. Put into separate bowls, adding 4 tablespoons salt to each. Stir, then leave for 30 minutes for the juices to run. At the end of this time, wash both aubergines and courgettes under the cold tap, drain and pat dry. plunge the tomatoes into boiling water to skin them, cut them across in half, remove the seeds and slice roughly. Put the peppers under the grill to skin them, slice lengthwise in two, remove the seeds and cut into strips. Cut the onions into quarters.

Pour a glass of olive oil into a fairly large frying pan and, over a high heat, colour the courgettes. Using a skimmer, transfer to a large casserole in which the ratatouille will be cooked. Repeat for the aubergines and then for the sweet peppers and onions. When all these vegetables are in the casserole, add the tomatoes, the rest of the oil, the bouquet garni and oregano, and the garlic cloves. Season with pepper, but not yet with salt. Cover the pan and put over a medium heat. When it has come to the boil, turn down the heat and simmer for at least 1 hour 30 minutes, stirring from time to time. By this stage, the ratatouille will have its characteristic appearance and flavour, and the vegetables will be cooked without disintegrating. Taste and season with salt and pepper. If the cooking has released a lot of liquid, take off the lid and reduce over a high heat, watching that the vegetables don't stick.

Serve hot as a vegetable, or cold, sharpened with a little lemon juice or vinegar or even a few drops of Tabasco sauce. The ratatouille will keep for several days in a well-sealed container in the refrigerator.

Fish and
Shellfish

Grilled sea bass

The sea bass, known in France as 'bar' on the Atlantic coast and 'loup' in the Mediterranean, is one of the finest sea fish. Grilling, with a garnish of aromatic herbs infused in olive oil, is both the simplest and most delicious treatment for it, as for the gilt-head bream and all the large colourful fish of the Mediterranean. A plain sauce is sufficient, made in a bain-marie with melted butter or olive oil, fennel seeds and lemon juice; beyond the Mediterranean region, a butter sauce is preferred, in the form of hollandaise or beurre blanc.

For 6   1 sea bass weighing 2–2.3 kg (4 lb 8 oz–5 lb 2½ oz)
fennel or coriander seeds, thyme, bayleaf
olive oil
twigs of rosemary and savory
2 lemons
salt, pepper

Ask your fishmonger to gut the fish through the gills, and to scale it, leaving the dorsal fin; it is by pulling this that you can tell whether the bass is cooked—it should come away with very little resistance. Steep the mixed herbs in a glass of olive oil for several hours, then drain and salt.

Heat the grill to the maximum temperature. Stuff the inside of the fish with 2 level tablespoons herbs, and dip in olive oil. Place on the grid of the grill pan or drip pan, make oblique gashes in the skin, and season with salt and pepper. Grill under a moderate heat or, if using an oven grill, positioned on the middle rung of the oven. Brush occasionally with olive oil, using the bunch of rosemary and savory. When the first side is golden, turn the fish over, place directly in the pan, and colour the other side. Then heat the oven to 200°C/400°F/Mark 6, turn off the grill, season the bass with salt and pepper and lemon juice, and finish cooking in the oven. Continue to baste with olive oil and cook until the dorsal fin comes away easily. During this time, you can make the sauce of your choice.

Steamed sea bass

In this recipe the fish is divided into portions, seasoned with salt and pepper, and it is cooked in a matter of minutes. With the natural action of the steam, the flesh remains firm, pearly and full of flavour. All you need is a large pan or pot with a lid, into which a colander or strainer will fit tightly; a couscoussier is ideal. You can experiment with any kind of white fish.

Scale the sea bass and remove the head, and cut into even portions. Strew a thin layer of fresh herbs in the bottom of the colander, using parsley on its own or with a few branches of chervil and tarragon. Place the fish on top, season with salt and pepper and cover with the lid. Pour enough water into the lower pan to come just below the level of the colander, add the colander and make sure that the join is watertight, if necessary tying round with a moist cloth. Bring the water to the boil and steam the fish for 20–25 minutes, depending on the size of the pieces. Check to see that the fish is done, and skin it. Serve on the bed of herbs, arranged on a napkin in a dish, and hand round whatever sauce you have chosen in a sauceboat.

Baked gilt-head bream with coriander

This recipe calls for fresh coriander leaves or 'Arab parsley'; you will find it in large towns and speciality grocers. However, as we are not very accustomed to the taste, it's a good idea—especially in a dish where no water is involved—to wring out the leaves, after chopping them, in a cloth or in kitchen paper. This is a simple little precaution to obtain one of the most delicate preparations of the eastern Mediterranean.

For 4–6   1 large, or 2 medium, gilt-head bream weighing 1.5 kg
              (3 lb 6 oz) altogether
              fresh coriander leaves
              4 lemons
              200 ml (⅓ pint; ⅞ cup) olive oil
              salt, pepper, paprika

Ask your fishmonger to gut the bream through the gills and scale it carefully. Wash the fish and pat dry. Season the inside fairly generously with salt and pepper, and insert a sprig of coriander. Make 3 shallow, slanting cuts on each side of the skin. Slice the lemons into rounds, and finely chop enough coriander to give 2 tablespoons.

Preheat the oven to 200°C/400°F/Mark 6. Cover the bottom of an ovenproof serving dish with a layer of lemon slices, and place the fish on top. Season with salt and pepper, sprinkle with a few pinches of paprika, surround with more lemon slices, and moisten with sufficient olive oil to give at least 1 cm (½ in) in the base of the dish. Put in the oven and, after 15 minutes, add the chopped coriander leaves to the hot cooking juices and lower the temperature to 160°C/320°F/ Mark 3. Continue to cook for another 40–45 minutes for one large fish, or 30–35 minutes for 2 medium ones, basting from time to time and making sure that the coriander does not burn. Then turn off the oven, cover the fish with a sheet of foil, and leave with the door half open until ready to serve; it will continue to cook and swell in its own heat.

Pasta with cockles

The disadvantage of this delicious shellfish is that it is often full of sand, which is not even removed by cooking. The solution is to open the cockles rapidly over the heat in a saucepan, shell them, place in a colander and rinse in cold water. The cooking juices are then carefully transferred to another pan, without disturbing the sediment, and the cockles returned to the liquid with a pinch of salt. In this way they lose none of their flavour.

For 6   2 litres (3½ pints; 4½ US pints) cockles
                 400 g (14 oz) thin noodles
                 1 tablespoon oil
                 50 g (1¾ oz; ¼ cup) butter
                 200 g (7 oz; ¾ cup) cream
                 40 g (1½ oz) Parmesan cheese
                 60 g (2 oz) grated Gruyère cheese
                 salt, pepper

Open the cockles over the heat and shell them. Pour their juices into another pan, leaving the sand and grit behind, and reduce to 4–5 tablespoons, no more. Cook the noodles in plenty of salted boiling water with the oil. As soon as they are cooked, but still firm—or 'al dente' as the Italians say—refresh in cold water to stop them cooking in their own heat, and drain thoroughly.

When the time comes to serve the dish, reheat the noodles in a large pan with the butter, cream, Parmesan, Gruyère, cockles and the reduced cooking liquid, adding the ingredients one after the other in the above order, and each time incorporating well and lifting the noodles with two forks to disentangle them. Heat until both noodles and cockles are thoroughly coated, taste and season with salt and pepper. Serve without delay. This delicious entrée can be served equally well at a dinner party as at a family meal. Mussels or shelled prawns can be prepared in the same way, although they don't have the same delicacy.

Crab salad with herbs

This calls for large crabs or spider crabs, mixed with a great variety of ingredients. It makes a cold entrée, or, followed by cheese, a meal in itself.

For 6

1 large or 2 medium crabs weighing 600–800 g (1 lb 5 oz–1 lb 12¼ oz) altogether
1 small tin of cooked chick-peas
1 small tin of sweetcorn
1 grapefruit
1 apple, or ½ small tin of pineapple chunks
1 lemon
1 head of celery
chives, parsley, mint, chervil
2 teaspoons mustard
1 onion
1 clove of garlic
1 tablespoon vinegar
6 tablespoons olive oil
1 teacup mayonnaise (see p. 58)
1 yolk of egg
250 ml (scant ½ pint; 1⅛ cups) groundnut oil
Tabasco sauce
1 lettuce
100 g (3½ oz) small black olives
a few radishes and small tomatoes (optional)
salt, pepper

If possible, buy live crabs and cook them yourself the day before. Weigh them separately and calculate the cooking time, at 10 minutes per 500g (1lb 2oz). Put them into a large stockpot, cover with cold water, season with salt, bring to the boil and cook for the required time. Then turn off the heat, take the lid off the pan and leave for 5 minutes before rinsing them under the cold tap. Crack open, extract all the meat and refrigerate in a sealed container overnight.

Drain the tins of chick-peas and sweetcorn, and pineapple, if used, in a colander, using only half of each tin. Peel the grapefruit, divide into segments, slicing down to remove the membrane, and then cut each into 2–3 chunks. Peel the apple, if used, and dice finely, sprinkling with lemon juice to prevent it turning brown. Separate out the nicest parts of the celery and the heart, and slice very thinly on a board. Cut up the chives and chervil, and chop the parsley and 8–10 leaves of mint. Make the vinaigrette with 1 teaspoon of the mustard, the chopped onion, the pressed or crushed clove of garlic, vinegar and olive oil. You don't have to make too much, as this is not the only dressing, but merely helps to bring out and heighten the flavours. Then mix all the prepared ingredients in a bowl, and keep in a cool place until ready to serve.

Just before serving, add the mayonnaise, the rest of the mustard, the egg yolk, groundnut oil, salt and pepper, and a few drops of Tabasco. Line a salad bowl with the large outer leaves of the lettuce, fill with the salad and scatter the olives on top. Decorate, if you like, with a few radishes and tomato slices and, if you are preparing the dish in advance, don't forget small lettuce leaves to garnish with.

Poached freshwater crayfish

This rare and expensive treat deserves to be well prepared. The best crayfish are the famous 'red legs', where the claws are not only coloured, but are larger and thicker than those of other types. They are served with their hot poaching liquid or court-bouillon, handed round separately in cups, while the crayfish themselves are cold, which makes the flesh firm and easier to extract from the shells.

For 6	36–40 freshwater crayfish (at least)
	2 carrots
	2 sticks of celery
	2 onions
	1 bottle of good quality white wine (Chablis or
	    Riesling)
	1 clove
	12 coriander seeds
	½ teaspoon mignonnette pepper (crushed white and
	    black peppercorns)
	12 fennel seeds
	1 small hot pepper
	1 bayleaf
	1 sprig each savory and thyme
	1 clove of garlic
	salt

Slice the carrots into thin rounds, cut the celery into dice, and slice the onions into rounds. Take a large pan into which the crayfish will easily fit, pour in 1 litre (1¾ pints; 2¼ US pints) water and the wine, and add the herbs and vegetables. Bring to the boil and cook for 20–25 minutes.

Meanwhile, wash and clean the crayfish, very gently extracting the central part of the tail and, with it, the black gut. Add the crayfish to the court-bouillon and, when it has come back to the boil, cook gently for 10 minutes. Then take out the crayfish and allow to cool. Strain the liquid, reserving a few rounds of carrot, return to the pan and reduce until you have about 6 teacups.

Serve hot or cold, as you wish, with 2–3 slices of carrot in each cup. This delicately-flavoured court-bouillon can also be served without reducing, and the leftovers used for poaching other fish like trout.

Eels 'au vert'

This delicious preparation, equally good cold or hot, is worth making in quantity. You can keep the leftovers for at least a week, in a covered glass dish or bowl, in the refrigerator (not the freezer).

For 6–8	2 kg (4 lb 8 oz) eels 3 medium onions 3 sticks of celery, or 50 g (1¾ oz) celeriac

200 g (7 oz) watercress leaves
2 tablespoons parsley
2 tablespoons chervil leaves
1 heaped tablespoon chives
15–20 mint leaves
1 sprig of thyme
1 sprig of savory
250 g (8¾ oz) sorrel leaves
50 g (1¾ oz; ¼ cup) butter
flour
1 bottle of white wine
4 yolks of egg
200 g (7 oz; ¾ cup) fresh cream
1 lemon
salt, pepper

Skin the eels and cut them into thick chunks. Chop the onions and celery together, or grate the celeriac. Wash the herbs and chop them all together. Pull out the stalks of the sorrel up to the middle of the leaf, and cut into fine strips. Reserve each ingredient, or mixture of ingredients, in its own dish.

Choose a saucepan large enough to hold everything, with, as far as possible, the slices of eel in a single layer. Soften the onions and celery in the butter over a moderate heat, stirring often to prevent them colouring. Flour the pieces of eel very lightly, shake off the excess, and add them to the pan. Seize them without browning over a high heat, put in the sorrel immediately and mix. Then moisten with three quarters of the wine, bring to the boil, and add the rest of the herbs and more wine if necessary so that everything is just covered. Cook at a steady boil, without a lid, for 12–15 minutes.

If you are serving the dish straight away, combine the eggs with the cream, plus a few spoonfuls of sauce, and add to the pan off the heat. Taste and correct the seasoning, and squeeze in a few drops of lemon juice if required. Reheat gently without boiling. If the dish has to wait, reheat just before serving without allowing it to boil furiously.

Conger eel soup with herbs

The conger is a long fish with a very delicate flavour and firm flesh. Although the tail end is very bony, the middle and neck contain far fewer bones and these can easily be extracted. Ask your fishmonger to cut you the slices from this part, one for each person, and about 1.5 cm (½ in) thick.

For 6
6 slices of conger eel
300 g (10½ oz) sorrel
1 fairly large bunch of parsley
1 bunch of chervil
2 onions
2 cloves of garlic
2 yolks of egg
125 g (4¼ oz; ½ cup) fresh cream
1 lemon
salt, pepper
bread

Pick over and trim the sorrel, pulling out the stalk as far as the middle of each leaf. Chop it together with the parsley and chervil, reserving a good pinch of chervil leaves for decoration at the end. Chop the onion and garlic very finely. Arrange the slices of eel in a single layer in a wide saucepan or stockpot, cover with the herbs and vegetables, pour on 2 litres (3½ pints; 4½ US pints) water, and season with salt and pepper.

Cook at a gentle boil for 30 minutes, then taste and correct the seasoning. To serve, put the egg yolks and cream in the bottom of the soup tureen, with the reserved chervil and 1 teaspoon lemon juice. Gradually add the soup by the ladleful, mixing it in, and then pour on the whole lot. For a special touch, slice the bread into rounds the same size as the fish, and toast. Place one in each bowl, followed by a slice of eel, and pour on the soup.

Baked red gurnard with anchovy butter

The red gurnard is a beautiful red fish, with a rounded body, a large spiky head and delicate flesh. It belongs to the Triglidae family, and has nothing to do with the red mullet, of the Mullidae family, except its colour. The medium-sized gurnard are cooked in the oven, while the larger ones are more often poached in a court-bouillon.

For 6   6 red gurnard weighing 250–300 g (8¾–10½ oz) each
                 2 teaspoons dried thyme
                 1 teaspoon fennel seeds
                 5 tablespoons olive oil
                 1 lemon
                 salt, pepper
                 anchovy butter (see p. 50)

Ask your fishmonger to gut the fish and remove the heads. Preheat the oven to 200°C/400°F/Mark 6. Make a bed of thyme and fennel seeds in an ovenproof dish, and arrange the fish on top, seasoned inside with salt and pepper. Sprinkle with the olive oil and lemon juice.

Put in the oven and, after 10–12 minutes, when the skin is beginning to dry out, baste the fish and lower the temperature to 180°C/350°F/Mark 4. Depending on the thickness of the fish, bake for 35–45 minutes, basting frequently and, if they are drying out too quickly, cover with foil. Serve in the same dish, and hand round the anchovy butter with it, at room temperature or melted in a bain-marie. Accompany with plain boiled potatoes.

Grilled herrings with sorrel sauce

Grilling is a good method for fresh herrings, making them less greasy and therefore more digestible; and, if you have an oven grill, there is very little smell. You can adapt this recipe for the barbecue, preparing the herrings in the same way: have handy some twigs of savory, rosemary and thyme, and throw them onto the charcoal from time to time—this will mask the unpleasant odour of the dripping fat, and also add flavour to the fish. Mackerel can be cooked in the same way and are also delicious.

For 6   6 fresh herrings weighing about 180 g (6¼ oz) each
                 oil
                 1 heaped teaspoon chopped shallot
                 2 teacups sorrel leaves cut into fine strips
                 1 tablespoon butter
                 1 teaspoon strong mustard
                 250 g (8¾ oz; 1 cup) cream
                 1 lemon
                 salt, pepper

Ask your fishmonger to gut the herrings through the gills, and to replace the soft and hard roes inside. Wipe the fish, brush lightly with oil, and make 3 slanting incisions on each side.

Preheat the grill 15–20 minutes before cooking. Place the herrings on the grid of the grill pan or drip pan, and grill slowly, with the door open if in the oven. As soon as they begin to colour, turn over at once before they curl up, and grill the other side a little longer so that the roes are cooked enough. Season with salt and pepper and leave under the grill which has been turned off, serving as soon as possible.

To make the sauce, finely chop the shallot and cut the sorrel leaves into thin strips (don't chop them). Soften the shallot in the butter over a very moderate heat without letting it brown. Then add the sorrel and, as soon as it is soft but still green, the mustard, mixing it in thoroughly, followed by the cream. Simmer without covering the pan, and squeeze in half the juice of the lemon. When the cream is smooth and thick enough to coat a wooden spoon, season with salt and pepper and taste. Keep hot without continuing to cook, and hand round in a sauceboat.

When available, serve new potatoes with the herrings. Choose small ones, cook them in their skins in salted water, then peel. Place them very hot in a serving dish, sprinkled with the sorrel sauce and scattered with a little finely chopped parsley or chervil.

Monkfish in paper cases

Monkfish or angler fish (known in France as 'lotte' or 'baudroie') is boneless. In this recipe, it is cut into slices 1–2 cm (½ in) thick, cooked in parcels of foil and flavoured with a herb butter. The method can be adapted for the barbecue, raking the ashes over the coals to moderate the heat, and turning the parcels to cook on both sides. Other fish can be cooked in the same way, including cod, hake, pike-perch, or fillets of gilt-head bream, whiting, and even sole.

For 6   about 1.2 kg (2 lb 11 oz) monkfish
               1 tablespoon bland oil
               2 tablespoons parsley
               2 medium onions
               2 shallots
               1 tablespoon chervil leaves

1 teaspoon thyme leaves
200 g (7 oz; ⅞ cup) salted butter
2–3 lemons
salt, pepper, cayenne pepper

Cut the monkfish into as many slices as there are diners, plus 2 extra. Put the oil into a frying pan and, over a brisk heat, sweat out the moisture from the fish and dry the surface; there may be a lot of liquid, or almost none, but the operation should be performed quickly. Remove the central cartilage from each slice, and fill the hole with the flesh from the extra slices.

Finely chop, separately, the parsley, onions and shallots, and incorporate into the butter, together with the chervil and thyme leaves, working with a fork. Season with pepper and a pinch of cayenne. Cut a square of foil and test it for size with one of the slices of monkfish; when you have got the dimensions right, cut 5 more squares. Place a round of lemon, a slice of fish and a good tablespoonful of herb butter on each square, fold up and seal tightly, without crushing the contents. Leave for 1–2 hours for the flavour to develop—in fact, this preparation can be done well in advance, even the day before and the parcels refrigerated overnight.

Preheat the oven to 200°C/400°F/Mark 6. Place the packets in a single layer in a baking pan or dish, and put in the oven. When you can hear the insides bubbling, turn off the oven and leave the parcels, still sealed, with the door ajar until the time comes to serve them. Accompany with boiled potatoes and the rest of the herb butter, melted in a bain-marie, and sharpened with a few drops of lemon juice.

Monkfish roasted like a leg of mutton

For this dish, you need the complete tail of a monkfish. Ask your fishmonger to divide the fish into slices on the bulging side, just cutting through the backbone without separating the slices. This will make serving easier, and will open the flesh up to the herbs so that it gains in flavour.

For 6	1 monkfish tail weighing 1.2–1.4 kg (2 lb 11 oz–3 lb 2 oz)
	2 cloves of garlic
	4 tablespoons parsley
	2 lemons
	400 ml (⅔ pint; 1¾ cups) olive oil
	12 large mussels
	1 level tablespoon fennel seeds
	salt, pepper

Lay out the monkfish in a long dish or roasting pan, with the sliced side on top, season with salt and pepper and leave until ready to cook. Preheat the oven to 250°C/500°F/Mark 10 or the maximum temperature. Chop the garlic and parsley quite finely, and slice one of the lemons into thin rounds. Slip a slice of lemon into each of the openings in the fish, sprinkle with 4 tablespoons oil and put in the oven. The first part of the cooking is to drive off the moisture, so wait a few minutes until all the liquid has been released, then pour it away; some monkfish don't sweat, so keep an eye open and don't let it dry out.

Now moisten with 6 tablespoons oil, put a pinch of parsley into each of the slits, and turn down the oven to 200°C/400°F/Mark 6, leaving the door half open for the first few minutes. Continue to cook, basting occasionally, allowing 20 minutes per 500 g (1 lb 2 oz). Arrange the mussels in a single layer around the fish 10–12 minutes before the end and, as soon as they have opened, sprinkle with the rest of the chopped garlic and parsley. Meanwhile, make the sauce by heating the rest of the olive oil with the fennel seeds in a bain-marie. Season with salt and pepper, squeeze in the juice of half a lemon, and add the flavoured cooking juices from the fish. Serve with plain boiled potatoes.

Red mullet with anchovy butter

Red mullet rank among the most delicate of fish, those of the Mediterranean being especially prized. Ask your fishmonger to gut them through the gills, and to reserve the livers for you. You can season these with salt and pepper and sprinkle with a few thyme leaves, then put them back inside the fish.

For 6   6 red mullet weighing 180–200 g (6¼–7 oz) each
               thyme, oregano or savory
               olive oil
               1 lemon
               parsley
               salt, pepper
               200 g (7 oz; ⅞ cup) anchovy butter (see p. 50)

Cut off the fins of the red mullet, except the dorsal fin by which you
can tell when the fish are cooked. Quickly wash the outside under the
cold tap, and dry with kitchen paper. Put the livers inside or, if you
have not kept them, season the interior with salt and pepper, and add
a few thyme leaves or a small bunch of oregano or savory—don't
worry if you can't get these fresh since the anchovy butter will give
enough flavour. Paint the fish on both sides with olive oil, and arrange
on the grid of the grill pan or roasting pan.

Preheat the grill for 15-20 minutes, then place the fish underneath.
In the case of an oven grill, position them on the third rung from the
bottom, and make sure that the door is open or half open. When the
skin is becoming puffy, take the fish out and turn them over carefully
without breaking, using a metal spatula. Brush again with oil, and
continue to cook until the skin starts to brown, when they should be
cooked. Check by pulling a bone from the dorsal fin, which should
come away easily, and don't delay in checking—it would be a pity for
the red mullet to overcook and dry out. Meanwhile, melt the anchovy
butter in a bain-marie, finely chop the parsley and slice the lemon into
rounds. Arrange the fish in a heated serving dish, and cover the heads
with a thin slice of lemon, sprinkled with parsley. Hand the anchovy
butter round in a sauceboat.

Mussels with basil

This is a mussel salad, served on a bed of curly endive or lettuce strips. In the winter, when fresh basil is hard to find, you can replace it with parsley, or a heart of celery chopped very fine.

For 6
3 litres (5¼ pints; 6½ US pints) small cultivated
  mussels
1 onion
1 tablespoon oil
½ teaspoon thyme
1 curly endive or lettuce
2 cloves of garlic
15–20 basil leaves
6 tablespoons olive oil
1 tablespoon vinegar
salt, pepper

Clean the mussels and chop the onion finely. Heat the oil in a wide pan and soften the onion and thyme. When they are just about to colour, put in the mussels and cover the pan. Open them over a high heat, shaking the pan so that the ones on top come to the bottom. When all have opened, shell them and allow to cool.

To make the sauce, pound the garlic and basil to a paste in a mortar. Bind with the olive oil, pouring it on in a thin stream and stirring all the time. Then add the vinegar, and season with salt and pepper. Pour over the mussels, mix together, and leave in a cool place for 20–30 minutes to allow the flavours to blend. Serve on a bed of curly endive or shredded lettuce.

Mussel soup

For this dish you should choose cultivated mussels, small but full, with tender flesh and a delicate taste. The large mussels, which are eaten raw in the south of France, are tougher and don't make a good soup.

For 6
1 litre (1¾ pints; 4½ cups) mussels
1 large or 2 small leeks
2 medium potatoes
30g (1 oz; ⅛ cup) butter
500 ml (scant pint; 2¼ cups) milk
1 teacup soft white breadcrumbs
2 tablespoons fresh cream (optional)
2 tablespoons chervil
salt, pepper

Clean the mussels by scraping the shells, and beard them, pulling off the tuft of fibre or byssus, which anchors them to their support in the sea. Do not soak them, but stir around rapidly in plenty of cold water, so that their sea water is not replaced by that from the tap. Put them in a large pan with half a glass of water, cover the pan and place over a high heat. After a few minutes, when the steam is escaping from the lid and the shells have opened, strain in a colander with a bowl below to collect the juices. Leave to cool a little, then shell and reserve.

Carefully decant the liquid into a jug, leaving the sediment behind. Slice the white part of the leeks into thin rounds, and do the same with the potatoes. Bring the milk to the boil in a saucepan, and keep hot.

Melt the butter until foaming in a large saucepan, add the vegetables and, over a fairly brisk heat, stirring often, soften without colouring. When they are giving off less steam, pour in the hot milk and the same amount of water, and add the breadcrumbs. Cook at a gentle boil for 30 minutes at the most, then purée in a vegetable mill or liquidizer, thinning with enough water to give the right consistency, and adding the mussel juices. Season with salt and pepper.

Just before serving, cut the chervil leaves into fine strips with scissors, rather than chopping, to preserve all the flavour. Reheat the soup with the mussels and cream (if used), sprinkle with the chervil, and serve in cups.

Grilled salmon

For this dish, you can use thick steaks of salmon, 100–120g (3½–4½oz) each, cut across and taken from the middle, or thin slices without bone, carved off on the bias like escalopes. However, the latter are more often fried in butter, while the steaks look more attractive criss-crossed with the pattern of the grill, and showing off their fine pink flesh. Hollandaise or béarnaise are the favourite sauces to serve with salmon, but you should not overlook other possibilities like beurre blanc (see p. 54), plain or discreetly flavoured with chervil or dill, or anchovy butter, or green herb butter (see p. 50 and 57).

For 6　　　　6 steaks of salmon weighing about 150–200g
　　　　　　　　 (5¾–7oz) each
　　　　　　butter or oil
　　　　　　salt, pepper

   Preheat the grill so that it is hot but not burning. Wipe the salmon steaks, dip them in melted butter or oil, and season on both sides with salt and pepper.

   Place under the grill and, when the surface is warm to the touch, the exposed side should be browned and marked with the pattern of the grill. Turn over carefully, without breaking, and quickly colour the other side. Don't overcook this beautiful fish, for the firm flesh can easily become dry. In fact, it's safer, if you lack experience, to simply grill the steaks to colour them, without worrying about the actual cooking; then place them in an ovenproof serving dish and put in a heated oven, with the door open, to finish cooking. Serve with the sauce of your choice. In Scotland, where salmon abounds, it is often accompanied by peas and small boiled potatoes.

Scallops in the traditional style

For 6　　　　12–18 scallops
　　　　　　2 medium leeks
　　　　　　2 shallots
　　　　　　40g (1½oz; generous ⅛ cup) butter
　　　　　　250ml (scant ½ pint; 1⅛ cups) dry white wine

250 g (8¾ oz; 1 cup) cream
2 yolks of egg
1 level teaspoon flour
golden breadcrumbs
salt, pepper

Ask your fishmonger to open the scallops, and make sure that he detaches the small, sand-filled sac from the orange coral and the white, frilly membrane. Allow 2–3 scallops per person, depending on their size and the amount of coral, and set aside 6 of the nicest shells, washing them carefully. Cut the white part of the leeks into chunks of 1 cm (½ in), and chop the shallots finely.

Melt the butter in a saucepan and gently cook the leeks and shallots. As soon as the leeks are done, pour in the wine, season with salt and pepper, and boil for 2 minutes. Then allow to cool slightly before adding the scallops, and bring slowly to a simmer. The scallops will be cooked in a few minutes, when the white flesh is opaque and milky. Remove them with a skimmer, and reduce the cooking juices at a steady boil until you have 3 tablespoons left. Heat the cream in a separate pan and cook at a rolling boil until it coats a wooden spoon. Mix the egg yolks with the flour so that there are no lumps, pour on the boiling cream and add the reduced cooking juices.

Arrange the scallops in the reserved shells, cover with the sauce, and sprinkle lightly with the breadcrumbs. Put under a moderate grill, or under the oven grill in the middle of the oven, to brown the surface slowly and gently and, at the same time, heat the scallops. Watch that the sauce does not boil, although the flour is there to prevent the egg yolks curdling if this should happen.

Scallops with butter

Fresh, live scallops are available during the months with an 'r' in their names (although from April to October they have no coral). You can also buy frozen scallops, but gourmets don't think much of them. Scallops are beautiful and delicious shellfish, but it is essential not to mask their flavour with overpowering herbs, or to kill it by overcooking. According to their size you should allow 4–5 scallops per person, or more for a party—extravagant, perhaps, but an outstanding dish for a special occasion.

For 6   24–30 scallops
              flour
              100g (3½oz; ½ cup) butter
              1 tablespoon chopped parsley
              salt, pepper
              lemons

Ask your fishmonger to open the scallops and shell them. Detach the black, sand-filled sac from the coral, and discard the white, frilly membrane. Wash the scallops, drain and pat dry. Separate the orange corals from the white flesh, and set aside to be cooked briefly at the end, so that they do not burst. Flour the white parts very lightly and shake off the excess.

Melt most of the butter in a frying pan and, as soon as it is foaming, put in the scallops. Cook over a very moderate heat, shaking the pan and turning the pieces, until the white flesh is opaque, which means that they are done. Continue to cook a little longer, if you like, to colour them, adding the corals and seasoning with salt and pepper 1–2 minutes before the end. Then sprinkle with the parsley, put in a large nut of butter, turn up the heat and sauté briskly. Take out the white parts first, arrange them in the centre of a heated serving dish and surround with the coral pieces. Pour over the buttery juices, which should be clear and a pale golden colour, and serve with slices of lemon on the table.

Place the scallops on a bed of stewed chicory with cream (see p. 115), and you have a very special dish. Or, if you chop a clove of garlic with the parsley and add to the frying pan at the end of the cooking time, you will have created Provençal-style scallops.

Queen scallops with snail butter

Queen scallops, mussels, Venus shells or cockles can all be prepared in the same way, with a fairly piquant snail butter.

For 6   100g (3½oz; ½ cup) salted butter
              2 tablespoons parsley
              2 shallots
              2 cloves of garlic
              pepper
              quatre-épices
              3kg (6lb 12oz) queen scallops

Prepare the snail butter (see p. 60) at least 30 minutes in advance, and reserve. Wash the queen scallops quickly in cold water, and drain. Open them over the heat, as for mussels. Add the snail butter, shaking the pan so that it melts, then take off the heat, put on the lid and leave for a few minutes to allow the flavours to develop. Serve with slices of crusty white bread, toasted and spread with butter.

Shellfish with Breton butter

All shellfish, even those you would normally eat raw, can be prepared in this way, and it makes a most acceptable little entrée. Cockles, mussels, clams and scallops can be served in the shell, or taken out of their shells and divided between small dishes or even tartlet cases, about six to each.

For 6　　　36–48 shellfish
　　　　　　2 cloves of garlic
　　　　　　2 shallots
　　　　　　2 tablespoons parsley
　　　　　　stale white bread
　　　　　　pepper, quatre-épices or mixed spices (pepper,
　　　　　　　　cloves, nutmeg and ginger)
　　　　　　1–2 tablespoons Muscadet
　　　　　　250 g (8¾ oz; 1⅛ cups) salted butter

One hour in advance, prepare the stuffing. Crush the garlic cloves, and finely chop the shallots and parsley. Remove the crusts from the bread, soak in water, then squeeze dry and shape into a small ball. Combine all these ingredients, plus the pepper and quatre-épices, and moisten with enough wine to make a smooth, blended paste, soft but not runny. Incorporate the softened butter, working together with a fork.

Preheat the oven to 250°C/500°F/Mark 10 or the maximum temperature. Open the shellfish and stuff with the savoury butter. Sprinkle a layer of salt 3–4 cm (1½ in) deep in the bottom of a dish or roasting pan, or small individual dishes, and put in the shellfish, wedging them in the salt. Bake until the butter is bubbling and brown, and serve piping hot with buttered slices of crusty white bread or toast. And drink the rest of the Muscadet!

Skate with brown butter

Skate or ray, like monkfish, is free of bones. Choose the thornback skate, which has a more delicate flavour and firmer flesh than the smooth-skinned type, and takes better to poaching in a court-bouillon. As for the brown butter, it is an alternative to the formidable black, or burnt, butter.

For 6
1.2–1.5 kg (2 lb 11 oz–3 lb 6 oz) thornback skate
1 sachet of powdered court-bouillon
4 tablespoons chopped parsley with a few tarragon leaves
200 g (7 oz; 7⁄8 cup) butter
1⁄2 glass cider vinegar
4 tablespoons capers
salt, pepper

Ask your fishmonger to divide the skate into large pieces, and wash them. Put into a large saucepan, sprinkle with the powdered court-bouillon and cover with cold water. Heat gently and simmer without boiling for 15–20 minutes, depending on the thickness of the fish. Then allow to cool slightly in the liquid, without a lid on the pan. Take out the pieces of skate, reserving the court-bouillon, and place on a board. Cut off the edges of the wings with a pair of scissors, and remove the skin with the bony 'bucklers', which look like buttons inlaid in the surface. Divide into portions, arrange in a serving dish, and sprinkle with the chopped herbs. Cover the dish and keep hot over a saucepan of hot water.

Melt the butter in a frying pan over a moderate heat, until it becomes a good, light-brown nut colour. Remove from the heat, slowly add the vinegar, pouring it into the edge of the pan, and the same amount of strained court-bouillon, then the capers. Return to the heat, bring to the boil and pour over the skate. Serve with steamed potatoes.

Creole-style skate

For 6
6–8 pieces of skate weighing 200 g (7 oz) each
2 medium onions
2 cloves of garlic

1 small red sweet pepper
1 bayleaf
2 sprigs each of thyme and parsley
6 tablespoons olive oil
2 tablespoons vinegar
cayenne pepper and saffron
6 tomatoes
400 g (14 oz; 1¾ cups) rice
salt, pepper

Ask your fishmonger to cut off the cartilaginous edges of the skate wings; he may also skin the fish for you. Wash the pieces and pat dry. Make a marinade 1–2 hours in advance. Chop one of the onions, crush the garlic, slice the pepper into fine strips, and put in a dish with the crumbled bayleaf, thyme, parsley, 4 tablespoons olive oil, the vinegar, salt, pepper and a pinch of cayenne. Leave the fish to marinate in this mixture.

Meanwhile, skin and de-seed the tomatoes, and chop roughly. Prepare the pilaff 45 minutes before serving, as the cooking time will vary with the quality of the rice and it doesn't matter if it is kept waiting. Measure out the rice into a bowl, pour 2½ times its volume of water into a pan, season with salt and a pinch of saffron, and bring to the boil. Chop the other onion, and soften without colouring in 2 tablespoons olive oil in a large saucepan. Add the rice all at once, stir, and cook until milky white. Then add 2 of the chopped tomatoes, cover with the boiling water and put the lid on the pan. Cook over a medium heat, without stirring, until the rice has absorbed all the water and the surface is full of holes. Still with the lid on, turn the heat right down and leave for 5–8 minutes for the rice to swell.

Pour off the marinade from the fish into a large heavy pan, add the rest of the chopped tomatoes and a small pinch of saffron, and cook over a high heat until the tomatoes are soft. Remove from the fire and allow to cool a little. Arrange the pieces of skate in a single layer in the sauce, if necessary adding 2 tablespoons water so that all are moistened. Cover the pan and simmer over a gentle heat for 40–45 minutes. Taste and correct the seasoning, which should be strong, and serve with the pilaff.

Fried lemon sole

For 6   3 lemon sole weighing 300–350 g (10½–12½ oz) each
breadcrumbs (see p. 56)
groundnut oil
salt, pepper
tartare sauce (see p. 63)

Ask your fishmonger to loosen both sides of the fish, without
skinning them, and to cut off the heads and tails. Wash them and pat
dry, season the flesh with salt and pepper, and reserve until ready to
cook.

Breadcrumb the fish just before frying. Pour the oil into a large
frying pan, to a depth of 2–3 cm (1 in), heat it and, when it is on the
point of smoking, add the fish skin-side down. Quickly seize, then
cook over a moderate heat until a beautiful pale golden. Drain on
kitchen paper and arrange on a hot serving dish. Serve with chips and
a bowl of tartare sauce.

Sole meunière

Sole, that wonderful fish which goes with any sauce, is never better
than when simply prepared 'à la meunière'. The whole secret lies in
the final cooking in clarified butter, after the preliminary frying in oil
or in oil and butter. Steaks of salmon, hake, cod or pollack can be
prepared in the same way.

For 6   6 sole weighing 180–200 g (6¼–7 oz) each
100 g (3½ oz; ¾ cup) flour
2 glasses of groundnut oil
200 g (7 oz; ⅞ cup) butter
3 lemons
2 tablespoons chopped parsley
salt, pepper

Ask your fishmonger to gut the sole and skin them on both sides.
Wash them quickly, pat dry, lay on a board and season with salt and
pepper.

Just before cooking, flour the sole and shake off the excess. Preheat the oven to 200°C/400°F/Mark 6. Cook the fish one at a time in 2 tablespoons oil, or half oil and half butter, in a frying pan over a brisk but not too high heat, until they are a nice golden colour; don't worry about the actual cooking, which will be completed in the oven. As each fish is ready, place it in a serving dish in the oven, leaving the door open.

When all the sole are done, pour off the fat from the frying pan and wipe it dry with paper towelling. Add the butter in pieces, and melt while shaking the pan. As soon as it begins to bubble, turn down the heat, skim and, when it is clear and transparent, pour over the fish. Season lightly with salt and pepper, and squeeze over a few drops of lemon juice. Decorate with the chopped parsley and thin slices of lemon, and serve with steamed potatoes.

Normandy fillets of sole

This combination of sole with mussels, and even shrimps, fine dry white wine and cream, in a smooth sauce made without flour, belongs to the modern tradition of great cookery. It can be applied to many other firm-fleshed fish, like sea trout, cod and pike-perch.

For 6
4 sole weighing 300–350 g (10½–12½ oz) each
1 litre (1¾ pints; 4½ cups) mussels
500 ml (scant pint; 2¼ cups) cream, preferably
    pouring cream
shrimps (optional)
salt, pepper

THE FUMET
500–600 g (1 lb 2 oz–1 lb 5 oz) fish bones and trimmings
1 onion
1 clove of garlic
1 bouquet garni
1 large carrot
salt
6 peppercorns
1 clove
1 bottle of Chablis or Muscadet

Ask your fishmonger to fillet the sole, and to give you the trimmings, except the skin. If necessary, make up the weight with trimmings and bones from other delicate fish—whiting, weever, gilt-head bream—to produce a fairly-bodied fumet. Put all the dry ingredients for the fumet in a saucepan, seasoning with a very little salt, then pour on the wine and enough water to cover the contents. Bring to the boil and cook for 20 minutes. Leave to cool and strain.

Preheat the oven to 180°C/350°F/Mark 4. Roll up the fillets of sole loosely, and secure with a cocktail stick. Arrange in an ovenproof dish, pour on the cooled fumet and season with salt and pepper. Cook in the oven for 10 minutes, so that the liquid is barely simmering. Then take out the fish and keep hot in a covered dish over a pan of hot water.

Open the mussels over the heat, reserving the juices. If you are using shrimps, shell them and swell by poaching briefly in hot, but not boiling, salted water. Meanwhile, reduce the fumet over a high heat and, before it reaches the stage of a syrup, add the mussel juices. Pour in the cream and cook until the sauce is thick and smooth and will coat the back of a spoon. Check the seasoning. Arrange the sole in a hot serving dish with the mussels and shrimps, and cover with the hot sauce. If the dish has to wait, protect the surface with a sheet of buttered paper and leave in a hot oven with the door open, making sure that it doesn't carry on cooking.

Squid in the style of Sète

Squid, or calamari, are molluscs in the shape of a horn, with very delicate flesh, whether large or small. In this recipe the body is cut into strips, and the head, which is the small beginning of the tentacles, is cleaned of the horny beak in the centre.

For 6
1.22 kg (2 lb 11 oz) small squid
2 medium onions
2 cloves of garlic
1 piece of orange peel
3 tomatoes
5 tablespoons olive oil
1 tablespoon tomato concentrate

150 ml (¼ pint; ⅝ cup) dry white wine
1 bouquet garni
1 yolk of egg
salt, pepper, cayenne pepper

Detach the head of each squid and remove the horny beak. Slit the body open, get rid of the grit and sand, and wash. Then cut into strips and pat dry. Chop the onions and garlic, and cut off a piece of orange peel the size of a middle finger. Skin and de-seed the tomatoes, and chop into bits.

Put 2 tablespoons olive oil into a thick-bottomed saucepan. Add the squid, and brown over a high heat until there is no oil left. Then put in the onions, garlic and orange peel, stir for 2 minutes, and add the tomatoes, tomato concentrate, white wine, bouquet garni, salt and pepper and a pinch of cayenne. The liquid should come just level with the contents of the pan, so top up if necessary with a little water or wine. Cover the pan and simmer over a low heat for 45 minutes at the most; do not overcook as this will toughen the squid.

Taste and correct the seasoning, which should be fairly piquant, and cook for a few more minutes if required. To thicken the sauce, beat the egg yolk with the rest of the oil, pouring it in a thin stream as for a mayonnaise. Cover the bottom of the serving dish with this mixture, and gradually thin with spoonfuls of the liquid from the squid. When it is a fairly elastic consistency, transfer all the rest of the squid stew to the serving dish, stirring all the time. Serve with rice or polenta, or even crushed semolina grain.

Trout with almonds

Today, this fine fish is mainly farmed or from the sea, not that it matters: it is still beautiful, appetizing and easy to handle, and does not require expert preparation.

For 6   100 g (3½ oz) flaked almonds
6 trout weighing 180–200 g (6¼–7 oz) each
flour
200 g (7 oz; ⅞ cup) butter
4 tablespoons groundnut oil
1 lemon
salt, pepper

First, brown the almonds. Spread them out on a baking sheet, and put in a medium oven (180°C/350°F/Mark 4) for just a few minutes, stirring frequently with a rubber spatula to avoid breaking them. Take out and reserve.

Ask your fishmonger to gut the trout through the gills. Wash and wipe them to remove any mud, but without tearing the skin. Season the insides with salt and pepper, and dip in the flour, shaking off the excess. Put 1 tablespoon each of butter and oil in a frying pan and, over a moderate heat, lightly colour the trout, 2 or 3 at a time according to the size of your pan. They should be a beautiful pale golden, but not completely cooked. As soon as they are ready, place in an ovenproof serving dish in a low oven to finish cooking through.

Melt the rest of the butter in a saucepan over a medium heat. Skim, and continue to cook so that the deposit falls to the bottom, without the butter changing colour. Then strain this clarified butter, and season with salt and pepper. Scatter the almonds over the trout, and sprinkle with the very hot clear butter and a few drops of lemon juice. Serve piping hot.

Poached trout

This dish is a useful expedient which many housewives don't know about: it makes an excellent start to a meal, whether elegant or informal. The trout can be served hot with a savoury butter, such as anchovy butter or beurre blanc (see p. 50 and 54), or melted butter sharpened with lemon juice; or cold with herb mayonnaise or tartare sauce (see p. 59 and 63)

For 6   6 trout weighing about 180 g (6¼ oz) each
                1 sachet of powdered court-bouillon

Ask your fishmonger to gut the trout through the gills. Wash them to get rid of all traces of blood from the inside, but don't attempt to remove the sticky slime, and be careful not to tear the skin.

Arrange the fish in a single layer in an oval casserole or long ovenproof dish, and sprinkle with the whole packet of court-bouillon. Pour on enough cold water to cover them by at least 1 cm (½ in). Bring slowly to the boil, without letting the water boil over, then immediately turn the heat right down, cover the pan and leave for 10–20 minutes, depending on the size of the fish, with the liquid barely moving. Remove from the heat and allow to cool a little. Then take out the trout one at a time, skinning them at once and placing on a serving dish, which should be heatproof if you are going to serve them hot.

Strain the cooking juices through a fine-meshed sieve, and sprinkle over the fish, not to cover them but simply to keep them moist. For serving hot, cover the dish with a sheet of foil, sealing as tightly as possible, and put in a hot oven (180°C/350°F/Mark 4) with the door open. They can wait there until ready to serve, without continuing to cook. When the time comes, pour off the liquid and serve the trout, glistening and firm. For serving cold, prepare them in the same way and refrigerate. They will keep without drying out for 48 hours, or even longer.

Indian-style tuna fish

The season for fresh tuna fish is a short one. But those large slabs of pink meat are very tempting, and they deserve to be cooked with care and delicacy. Prepared Indian-style, tuna is equally good hot or cold.

For 6
1 thick slice of tuna fish weighing 1.3–1.5 kg
   (2 lb 14½ oz–3 lb 6 oz)
1 small tin of anchovy fillets in oil
1 small bunch of thyme
2 bayleaves
½ bottle dry white wine
2 good carrots
3 onions
3 tomatoes
2 tablespoons olive oil
1 tablespoon curry powder
a pinch of saffron
a dash of cayenne pepper, or 1 small hot pimento
1 sugar lump
3 cloves of garlic
1 lemon
salt
rice

One hour in advance, drain the anchovy fillets, roll them up on themselves, and lard the slice of tuna with them. Place in a dish with the thyme and bayleaves, cover with the white wine, season lightly with salt and leave to marinate.

Meanwhile, dice the carrots very finely and slice the onions. Skin and deseed the tomatoes. Take a large oval casserole into which the tuna will fit, and sweat the carrots and onions gently in 1 tablespoon of the olive oil. Before they have taken colour, add the tomatoes and sprinkle with the curry powder and saffron. Season with the cayenne or pimento, and simmer. Drain and wipe the tuna fish, and brown lightly on both sides in the rest of the oil in a frying pan. Transfer to the casserole, pour on the marinade, add the sugar and garlic, and cover the pan. Simmer over a very low heat for 1 hour 30 minutes.

To serve, take out the tuna fish without breaking it, skin, and place on a serving dish. Pour off the fat from the casserole, and sharpen the sauce with the juice of half a lemon. Taste and correct the seasoning if necessary, and pour over the tuna. Serve with plain or saffron rice, that is, cooked in boiling water with a pinch of saffron so that it is a pale yellow.

Turbot with shallots

All those fish which usually need to be cooked in special saucepans become more manageable if the fishmonger takes out the backbone and the fins from the edges. They can then be cooked in a flat dish, or even a roasting pan. Turbot is best cooked in the oven: the flesh remains firm and delicious. The cooking time is 40–50 minutes at the most for a fish of 2 kg (4 lb 8 oz).

For 6   1 turbot weighing about 1.8 kg (4 lb)
3 tablespoons chopped shallots
80 g (2¾ oz; ⅜ cup) butter
300 g (10½ oz; 1¼ cups) cream
1 lemon
salt, pepper

Ask your fishmonger to remove the backbone and the fins at the edges through the black side. Chop the shallots and soften them over a gentle heat in half the butter until they are cooked but not coloured. Season with salt and pepper.

Preheat the oven to 200°C/400°F/Mark 6. Spread the shallots all over the inside of the turbot, and reshape it to fit your dish or roasting pan. If you have to use the latter, line it first with a sheet of foil, so that you can lift out the fish whole, without breaking it. Place the turbot in the dish or pan, with the black skin down, smear with the rest of the butter and season with salt and pepper. Put in the oven, and keep an eye on it at the beginning. Have ready the cream, seasoned with salt and pepper and sharpened with lemon juice. As soon as some juices form in the bottom of the dish, add a little of the seasoned cream and, at intervals throughout the cooking, add the remaining cream, 2–3 spoonfuls at a time, and baste. The cream will gradually thicken as you add it, whereas if it is all poured in at once at the beginning, it would remain liquid and ringed with fat. Take care trve the cream is only

just starting to colour when the turbot is cooked. Sein the same dish, or transfer from the roasting pan to another dish, and accompany with steamed potatoes sprinkled with parsley.

Baked freshwater fish

This easy recipe is good with small pike—not more than 1 kg (2 lb 4 oz)—as well as with trout or sea trout.

> 1 pike weighing about 1 kg (2 lb 4 oz)
> 2 tablespoons chopped shallots
> 100 g (3½ oz; ½ cup) butter
> 150 g (5¼ oz; ⅝ cup) cream
> 1 lemon
> 1 tablespoon each parsley and chervil
> salt, pepper

Preheat the oven to 200°C/400°F/Mark 6. Chop the shallots, and soften in half the butter in a saucepan over a moderate heat, without colouring. Spread them over the base of an ovenproof dish, cut the pike into thick steaks (not small rounds), and place on top. Dot with the rest of the butter.

Put in the oven and, after about 20 minutes, when the skin has lost its shine and dried out and is beginning to cook, baste with the cream, seasoned with salt and pepper and sharpened with 1 teaspoon lemon juice. Turn down the oven to 180°C/350°F/Mark 4, and continue to cook, basting two or three times. As soon as the cream has thickened, turn off the oven, sprinkle the dish with the herbs, and leave for a few minutes with the door half open. Serve with sauté potatoes, cut very small, or cooked cucumber.

Barbecue-grilled fish

To cook small fish like sardines, mackerel and herring, arrange them on a fine metal grid which is placed on top of the main barbecue grill. For cooking large fish whole, however, you will need a hinged double grill or wire basket, so that they can be turned over; or, alternatively, you can cut them into fairly thick slices—2–3 cm (1 in)—and treat like small fish. In any case, I would recommend adding a bunch of aromatic herbs to the charcoal—fennel, savory, oregano, thyme or even bayleaves—which will give a delicious scent at the end of the cooking time.

LARGE FISH
Ask your fishmonger to gut the fish through the gills. Do not scale it, and all the juices will be sealed in during cooking; the skin will be loosened by the steam and can easily be removed at the end, before dividing into portions. Season the inside with salt and pepper and, 15 minutes before cooking, brush both sides with oil, repeating when you put the fish on the barbecue.

To check whether the fish is cooked to perfection, lift one of the dorsal fins, which should come away easily; or insert the pointed blade of a knife along the fin as far as the backbone, and it should slide in without resistance. Serve with a cold sauce, such as aïoli (see p. 49) or mayonnaise flavoured with Tabasco sauce (see p. 59), or a hot sauce. The simplest hot sauce is made by heating butter or olive oil in a bain-marie, without boiling, and adding crushed fennel seeds, salt and pepper, lemon juice, and even finely pounded anchovy fillets.

SMALL FISH
Clean and gut the fish as necessary, and scale herrings, red mullet etc. You can leave the scales on sardines, if you prefer, and you will find that it keeps the flesh juicy and the skin comes off like a pea-pod after cooking. Similarly, with trout, the thick, slimy skin retains the juices; just make a gash on each side at the base of the tail and head, without

cutting the flesh, to allow the steam to escape and prevent the fish bursting.

For small fish as well, add a bunch of aromatic herbs to the charcoal when you turn them. Serve them simply with lemon juice and toast spread with salted butter; or the sauces for large fish go very well with mackerel, herring and trout.

Fish soup of the Midi

This is a homely soup, and economical; but it is so colourful, so delicious and so full of flavour, that its very aroma gives a lift to the heart like the Provençal sun.

For 6
1 conger eel head
3–4 pollack heads
1 weever
1 red gurnard
4 onions
6–7 cloves of garlic
200 ml (⅓ pint; ⅞ cup) olive oil
2 bayleaves
5 sprigs of thyme
1 piece of fresh or dried orange peel
a small pinch of rosemary
4 medium potatoes
½ teaspoon saffron
2 small hot pimentos
salt, pepper
1 long French loaf
1 small bowl of aïoli (see p. 49)

Remove the gills and eyes from the fish-heads, cut into pieces and wash, along with the whole fish. Chop the onions. Heat half the olive oil in a large, thick-bottomed saucepan or stockpot, add the onions and 3 whole garlic cloves, and soften without colouring, stirring all the time. Drain the fish and put them in the pan, turn up the heat and brown lightly, stirring until the flesh has come away from the bones and they are reduced to a thick mass. Pour on 2 litres (3½ pints; 4½ US pints) water, add the bayleaves, thyme, rosemary and orange peel, the thickness of a finger, and bring to the boil. Cook at a rolling boil for 20 minutes, season lightly with salt, and strain, pressing to extract all the juices.

Slice the potatoes into quite thick rounds, and crush 1 garlic clove. Add to the rinsed-out pan with the rest of the olive oil and the saffron, and heat while stirring until the potatoes are coloured yellow with the saffron. Then pour on the fish stock, if necessary topping up with a little water to get the amount you want. Season with salt and pepper, add the crushed pimentos, and boil fast until the potatoes are cooked.

Meanwhile, slice the loaf and, rather than toasting it, dry out in the oven. Rub with the rest of the garlic, and have the aïoli ready. When the soup is done, carefully thin the aïoli with a few spoonfuls of the hot liquid, and pour into the bottom of the soup tureen. Ladle in the rest of the soup, mixing all the time, and serve with the garlic bread on the table.

Marmite dieppoise

Each maritime province of France has its fish soup, and the marmite dieppoise comes from the Caux area of Normandy. Less famous than bouillabaisse, it nevertheless has a distinguished place among French regional recipes.

For 6–8   1 turbot or brill weighing about 500 g (1 lb 2 oz), or the same weight of monkfish
1 sole weighing 300–400 g (10½–14 oz)
1 red gurnard weighing about 350 g (12½ oz)
3 red mullet, or 2 grey gurnard
1 whiting
1 litre (1¾ pints; 4½ cups) mussels
2 tablespoons powdered court-bouillon
2 shallots
1 medium leek
150 g (5¼ oz) button mushrooms
1 medium onion
100 g (3½ oz; ½ cup) butter
150 g (1¾ oz; ⅜ cup) flour
1 bouquet garni
3 egg yolks
200 g (7 oz; ¾ cup) fresh cream

1 lemon
1 tablespoon chopped parsley
1 tablespoon chervil leaves
fried bread cubes
salt, pepper

All the fish listed are the classic mixture for the recipe, although the turbot can be replaced by slices of monkfish and the delicate red mullet by grey gurnard. However, the sole must be included. Ask your fishmonger to skin the sole and turbot or brill, to cut off the heads of the red mullet and gurnard, and to give you all the trimmings, together with the whiting, as a basis for the stockpot. Cut the fish into thick steaks, keeping the backbones; and the monkfish, if used, into slices 1 cm (½ in) thick. Place the fish heads and trimmings and the whiting in a large saucepan with 2.5 litres (4½ pints; 5½ US pints) water and the powdered court-bouillon. Bring to the boil and cook for 20 minutes, then strain, pressing well in the sieve to extract all the juices.

Chop the shallots, the white part of the leek, the mushrooms and onion. Melt 2 tablespoons butter in a stockpot, add the vegetables and cook without colouring for 5–7 minutes, stirring all the time. Then sprinkle with 3 level tablespoons flour, and cook for 2 minutes, mixing well. Pour on the strained fish stock, bring to the boil, add the bouquet garni and cook at a gentle boil for 10–12 minutes. Meanwhile, open the mussels over the heat, remove half the shell from each, and set aside. Carefully pour the mussel juices into the stockpot, leaving the sediment behind, then strain the stock through a fine-meshed sieve. The stock should now be smooth and thick, but not all flour has the same thickening power. If it is too liquid, thicken with 1 tablespoon butter worked with 1 tablespoon flour, adding it off the fire in small bits and mixing in. Then return to the heat and bring back to the boil.

When the stock is the right consistency, season with salt and pepper and put in the fish, placing the more delicate ones, like the red mullet, on top. Reheat until the liquid is barely simmering and cook gently for 30 minutes, without allowing to boil, which would spoil the look of the fish. Just before serving, add the mussels, then take out the fish with a skimmer, arrange in a serving dish and keep hot. Beat the egg yolks with the cream and the juice of half the lemon, mix into the stock, bring to the boil and pour over the fish. Sprinkle with the chopped parsley and chervil leaves, and garnish with small cubes of fried bread. If you want a vegetable accompaniment, you might consider small new potatoes, plainly boiled, or sautéed cucumbers (p. 116).

Terrine of fish in jelly

This is an entrée for a special occasion. It should be made in a glass mould, so that you can see how it is constructed and how it will look when unmoulded. The fish are arranged in layers, separated by a bed of various herbs, and sealed with a flavoured jelly. You can add to the fish specified in the recipe, or replace them, with salmon, pike-perch and trout: or use a single large fish.

For 8–10   1.5 kg (3 lb 6 oz) trimmed fillets of white fish—brill, John Dory, sole, whiting, weever, in equal amounts
1 egg
4 leaves of gelatine
500 ml (scant pint; 2¼ cups) chopped herbs—chervil, tarragon, chives, parsley, watercress, in equal amounts; plus 3 tablespoons extra chopped mixed herbs to flavour the mayonnaise
salt, pepper
1 lettuce
tomatoes (optional)
mayonnaise (see p. 58)
milk

THE FUMET
1.2 kg (2 lb 11 oz) trimmings of fine fish
1 bouquet garni (parsley, thyme, bayleaf)
2 medium carrots
2 onions
2 cloves
2 cloves of garlic
1 leek
4 sticks of celery
salt, pepper

Ask your fishmonger to fillet the fish and to give you the trimmings. First, make the fish fumet, which will be used for cooking the fish and for the jelly. Pour 3 litres (5¼ pints; 6½ US pints) water into a saucepan, add the bouquet garni, carrots, onions stuck with the cloves, garlic, green part of the leek, and celery, and bring to the boil. Cook steadily for 15–20 minutes, then add the fish trimmings. Skim and cook for 30 minutes at a gentle boil, in order not to disturb the liquid or make it cloudy. Then allow to cool slightly, and strain, without pressing the residue through the sieve. There should be about 2 litres (3½ pints; 4½ US pints) fumet. Taste and season with salt and pepper.

To cook the fish, take a sauté pan or wide, shallow saucepan, pour in almost half the fumet and season with salt and pepper. Heat until the liquid is barely simmering, and keep it like that as you add the fish one after the other, starting with the more firmly-fleshed brill and John Dory, and following with the sole, whiting and weever. Keep an eye on them, and take them out when they are cooked but still firm. Allow to cool.

To make the jelly, strain the cooking liquid from the fish into another pan, and pour on the rest of the fish fumet to give about 750 ml (1¼ pints; 3¼ cups). Boil over a high heat for 10–12 minutes to reduce, then remove from the fire. If the liquid is very cloudy, you can clarify it as follows: add a white of egg, whisked softly but not to a snow, and the egg shell, crushed finely in your hand; boil gently without stirring, and the impurities will rise to the surface, clinging to the egg white and shell; skim off the largest bits, then strain through a fine conical sieve or muslin. Soften the gelatine in cold water, and add to the fumet, reheated but not boiling. Stir until it is dissolved, then allow to cool.

Chop the herbs together roughly, put in a strainer and quickly pour through at least 1 litre (1¾ pints; 4½ cups) boiling water. Leave to drain thoroughly, if necessary wringing in a cloth. This is so that they do not spoil the terrine by fermenting in contact with the fish.

To assemble the terrine, first coat the bottom of the mould with the liquid jelly, about 1 cm (½ in) deep. Refrigerate to set. Cut the fillets of sole into diamond shapes, and arrange them decoratively on top of the jelly. Sprinkle with a layer of the herbs, cover with more jelly without disturbing the layers, and put back in the refrigerator to set. Then build up the rest of the terrine in alternate layers—the various fish, and the herbs moistened with a little cold liquid jelly. Finish with a layer of the fish, but do not tap the sides of the mould to settle the contents. Finally, cover with more jelly, pouring it in slowly so that it fills all the holes and corners. Put a board with a weight on top, and refrigerate for 6–8 hours, along with the rest of the jelly.

To serve, make a bed of lettuce leaves in a serving dish, and unmould the terrine on top. Decorate with the rest of the jelly cut into small cubes and, if you like, with some slices of tomato for a touch of colour. Have ready a fairly strong mayonnaise, thinned with a little milk and flavoured with 3 tablespoons chopped herbs. Hand this round at the same time. If you want to add more colour to the terrine, you should choose lobster, langoustine or other crustaceans, which keep for the same length of time as white fish; avoid using shellfish.

Meat

Barbecue cooking

The most common fuel for the barbecue is charcoal. Although it is simple to use, it is essential to get the method right: The embers must be glowing all over and beginning to develop a dusty coating of grey ash. If you are lucky enough to live in a wine-growing region, or are, perhaps, camping there, try to get hold of some bundles of vine branches for the barbecue. Light them in advance and wait until they have finished burning, then level off the surface, which will have started to glow and form a covering of ash. Oil the grill before you put on the meat or fish. And throw a few boughs of aromatic herbs on the cinders at the end of cooking; they will give a beautiful scent and flavour, far superior to the faggot of fennel dipped in alcohol which is used in restaurants to flambé fish.

Spit-roasting is also very popular with a barbecue, especially if there is a vertical spit, which prevents the fat falling onto the embers and giving off an unpleasant smell. Whether it is a chicken, a leg of lamb, pork, or top rump of beef, put a drip pan underneath; you can then baste during cooking with a marinade made of various herbs steeped in a mixture of oil and vinegar or lemon juice, and seasoned with salt and pepper and perhaps a dash of cayenne.

In the country you might have a barbecue grill or spit in the fireplace. In this case, the same principles apply as for charcoal or vine branches. The watchword is no flames, no fumes from the fire, and a container for the noxious tarry deposits.

Daube of the 'gardians'

'Gardians' are the mounted herdsmen or cowboys who look after the bulls of the Camargue; and the daube is a preparation of beef in wine sauce typical of southern France. Versions of the slow-cooked beef stew are known under other names, such as bourguignon or boeuf bourguignonne, and in Flanders, where the wine is replaced by beer, as carbonnade. All call for the use of culinary herbs, with their powerful flavour and healthful properties.

For 6   1.8–2 kg (4 lb–4 lb 8 oz) beef from the top rump or shin
1 bouquet garni of parsley, thyme, bayleaf, with a
    sprig of marjoram and 4 sage leaves
salt, 10 peppercorns
1 bottle of Côtes-du-Rhône
1 piece of salt pork rind
500 g (1 lb 2 oz) onions
500 g (1 lb 2 oz) tomatoes
2–3 cloves of garlic

Do your shopping the day before, leaving time to marinate the meat overnight. Cut the meat into even cubes, and put it in an earthenware or glass dish with the bouquet garni, salt, peppercorns and red wine. Leave in the marinade for the night.

Trim the fat from the pork rind, and place, skin side up, in the bottom of a heavy casserole. Finely slice the onions, and skin, de-seed and dice the tomatoes. Strain the meat from the marinade, and put in the casserole in alternate layers with the onions. Finish with the tomatoes, and bury the bouquet garni and garlic cloves in the middle. Pour on the strained marinade, if necessary adding a little water to come level with the surface. Start off over a high heat to bring to the boil, then cover the pan and continue to cook gently for 4 hours. Serve with steamed potatoes, or pasta with butter.

Cold jellied daube

This the model dish suitable for any season and for the holidays: it can cope with unexpected visitors or wait for late arrivals. It is a genuine beef pâté in jelly, and is cooked without any attention, except to make sure that it is cooked slowly, over a gentle heat. The natural accompaniment is a green salad, but a dish of hot chips handed round at the same time is always well received.

For 6–8   1.5–2 kg (3 lb 6 oz–4 lb 8 oz) top rump or shoulder of
    beef
2 calves' feet
250 g (8¾ oz) smoked belly pork

1 fairly large bouquet garni of parsley, thyme, bayleaf, and 2 sprigs of marjoram
250 g (8¾ oz) carrots
6 shallots
2 cloves of garlic
10 peppercorns
10 coriander seeds
2 cloves
a pinch of nutmeg
500 ml (scant pint; 2¼ cups) dry white wine
3 tablespoons olive oil
250 g (8¾ oz) onions
100 g (3½ oz) green olives (optional)
salt

Cut the beef into fairly large chunks—80 g (2¾ oz) each; split the
calves' feet in half, and cut the pork into wide strips. Slice the carrots
lengthwise, and slice the shallots. Put all the meat into an earthenware dish with the bouquet garni, carrots, shallots, whole garlic
cloves, peppercorns, coriander seeds, cloves and nutmeg. Pour on
the wine and add 1 tablespoon oil, and leave to marinate for 24 hours
in a cool place, stirring two or three times.

When the time comes to cook the daube, blanch the calves' feet by
plunging into strongly salted boiling water and leaving for 10 minutes
after it has come back to the boil. Then drain. Turn the contents of
the earthenware dish into a colander, set over a bowl to collect the
marinade, and reserve all the ingredients. Pick out the beef, wipe dry,
and brown in the rest of the oil in a large casserole, over a moderate
heat so that the oil does not burn. Chop the onions and add them,
along with the calves' feet and the marinade with all its vegetables and
seasonings, including the carrots. Bring to the boil, cover the pan and
cook gently for 1 hour. Then add enough boiling water to cover the
contents of the casserole, cook for a further 2 hours, taste and season
with salt—the daube should be highly seasoned.

When the meat on the calves' feet is coming away from the bones of
its own accord, the daube is done. Leave to cool slightly, still with the
lid on, then transfer to a dish so that you can disentangle the pieces of
meat more easily. Put them, with the carrots, in a glass or earthenware mould, and distribute the olives among them, previously stoned
and blanched for 5 minutes in boiling water. Strain the liquid from the

daube, and pour into the mould so that it penetrates right to the bottom and fills in any gaps. Cover with a board with a weight on top and, once the daube has completely cooled, refrigerate for 8 hours. Keep the surplus juices in the refrigerator as well, then remove the fat and cut the jelly into dice. Serve the daube by unmoulding on a bed of lettuce, and decorating with the cubes of jelly.

The chef's roast beef

This roast beef can wait on the guests and still be cooked to perfection, in other words hot in the centre but rare: in my opinion it's the only method which doesn't test the nerves of the hostess. Try it.

For 6   1–1.2 kg (2 lb 4 oz–2 lb 11 oz) rump steak, in the shape
               of a thick slab and without barding fat
           groundnut oil
           1 kg (2 lb 4 oz) courgettes (squash)
           125 g (4¼ oz; ½ cup) butter
           a pinch of thyme
           6 tomatoes
           3 tablespoons stale white breadcrumbs
           4 tablespoons chopped parsley
           1 small clove of garlic (optional)
           salt, pepper

Smear the meat by hand with just enough oil to grease the surface, and season on both sides with salt and pepper. Heat a frying pan without any fat, and lightly brown the joint on all sides, working fast over a high heat. Then place in an ovenproof dish, and leave until the last guest has arrived, or the beginning of the meal if there is a first course.

Wash and wipe the courgettes, without peeling them, and cut into dice. Colour them in a frying pan in a mixture of half oil and butter, stirring often and not letting them burn. Season with salt and pepper and the thyme, and keep hot in a serving dish. Cut the tomatoes in half across, remove the seeds, sprinkle with salt and leave for 5 minutes. Then turn them over to drain. Cover with a mixture of the breadcrumbs and parsley, and pressed garlic if used; place in a roasting pan and put in the oven, heated to the maximum temperature. Take them out as soon as they begin to turn golden, and arrange in the serving dish around the courgettes, keeping them hot.

Now put the meat into the very hot oven and cook for 12–15 minutes, turning half way through. Slip the courgettes and tomatoes into the oven when you take out the joint, and carve it in the cooking dish. Add the rest of the butter in pieces to the meat juices, season with salt and pepper, and shake the dish as it melts to form a smooth sauce.

Cold jellied lamb or kid

The meat of goat kid, killed young, is comparable to rabbit, only more delicate. Its season is the spring, just when herbs are at the peak of their flavour, before the plants reach maturity. This savoury preparation can be served as an hors d'oeuvre on its own, or as a main course with chips and a green salad.

For 6–8   2.5–3 kg (5 lb 10 oz–6 lb 12 oz) pieces of lamb or kid
from the scrag end, shoulder and middle neck
4 cloves of garlic
2 tablespoons chives
1 bayleaf
1 heaped teaspoon dried thyme leaves
3 tablespoons parsley
2–3 leaves of mint
500 ml (scant pint; 2¼ cups) dry white wine
500 ml (scant pint; 2¼ cups) degreased bouillon
powdered gelatine
salt, pepper

Before starting, choose an ovenproof dish into which the meat will fit snugly, and which is suitable for putting in the refrigerator and for presenting at table. Crush the garlic with the garlic press, or by using the blade of a knife on a board. Cut up the chives finely with scissors, crumble the bayleaf, chop the parsley finely with the mint. Mix all the herbs together, including the thyme.

Preheat the oven to 180°C/350°F/Mark 4. Arrange the pieces of meat in layers so that they overlap without crowding, sprinkle each layer with the herbs, and season lightly with salt and pepper. Pour on the white wine, and top up with enough bouillon to cover the meat. Put the lid on, and place in the oven to cook for about 2 hours 30 minutes; check to see that the liquid does no more than simmer very gently.

When it is cooked, take out of the oven and cover with the rest of the bouillon, with the gelatine dissolved in it. Leave to cool overnight without covering. Then remove the fat from the surface, cover with jelly and let it set in a cool place. Cover the dish and refrigerate to serve cold.

Neck of lamb with herbs

Neck, or scrag end, of spring lamb is a delicate, juicy morsel, which is worth preparing as a sauté. It is also one of the cheaper cuts of meat.

For 6   1.2–1.5 kg (2 lb 11 oz–3 lb 6 oz) scrag end of lamb
1 tablespoon oil
5 tablespoons white wine
5 tablespoons beef consommé
1 bouquet garni including a sprig of fresh mint
12 spring onions
2 leeks
50 g (1¾ oz; ¼ cup) butter
1 tablespoon chervil leaves, or a few leaves of basil
salt, pepper

Preheat the oven to 200°C/400°F/Mark 6. Put the oil in a frying pan, and lightly colour the pieces of lamb, transferring them to an oven-proof dish as they are ready. Season with salt and pepper, add the bouquet garni, and pour on the white wine and consommé. Put in the oven to finish cooking, turning the pieces from time to time.

Finely slice the onions, including their green tops, and cut the white part of the leeks into chunks of 1 cm (½ in). Over a very low heat, sweat them in the butter, to soften without browning. Just before serving, add the chervil or basil, cut with scissors, and turn onto the lamb, together with the cooking butter. Serve at the same time an assortment of new vegetables, fresh broad beans, or small glazed carrots (see p. 113).

Lambs chops with thyme

A barbecue of vine branches, in a large airy kitchen or in the garden, is ideal for grilling meat although very few cooks are lucky enough to have such an arrangement. However, a drop of oil in the frying pan, a pinch of thyme and perhaps two or three whole garlic cloves . . . try it—it's not bad at all.

For 4   4 chops or 8 cutlets of young lamb
            1 tablespoon bland frying oil (groundnut or corn)
            1 teaspoon thyme leaves
            2–3 cloves of garlic (optional)
            salt, pepper

Take a large frying pan, wide enough to hold the chops in a single layer, and put in the oil, using a type which does not burn at high temperatures. Sprinkle with the thyme, add the whole garlic cloves, if used, and heat without smoking over a brisk fire. Add the chops and colour on both sides, watching that the oil does not burn. Season with salt and pepper.

People have their own personal taste as to how well done they like their chops, or any grilled meat. Cook them accordingly, for a longer or shorter time, but do not attempt to cook them more slowly or quickly. In this recipe, the thyme gives an indication of the correct temperature, as it must not burn.

Roast noix of lamb

In this recipe, the 'noix' is taken from the centre of the shoulder, boned and tied into a flat, slab shape. This manner of presenting a roast shoulder, flavoured with bayleaf, thyme and rosemary, makes an elegant and very tasty dish

For 6   2 noix of lamb or young mutton weighing 700–800 g
                 (1 lb 9 oz–1 lb 12¼ oz) each
            bayleaves, thyme, rosemary
            50 g (1¾ oz; ¼ cup) butter
            1 clove of garlic (optional)
            salt, pepper

Ask your butcher to bone out the centre of the shoulders, and to tie them into flat slabs. Weigh each one and calculate the cooking time at 20 minutes per 500 g (1 lb 2 oz) for the thickest one. One hour before cooking, season on both sides with salt and pepper and, for each noix, insert under the string 2 bayleaves, a few sprigs of thyme and a sprig of rosemary.

Preheat the oven to 220°C/425°F/Mark 7 for 15 minutes. Place the noix on the metal grid of the roasting pan, put in the oven and, when the first side is nicely browned, turn over and add half a glass of water to the pan. Finish the cooking, then leave for 5 minutes with the oven off and the door half open. Carve into slices, saving the juices. Deglaze the pan with 1 tablespoon boiling water and the butter, scraping up the bits with the back of a fork, pour in the juices from the carving, and hand round in a heated sauceboat. If you like garlic, squeeze a drop or two into the hot sauce with the garlic press as a finishing touch.

Roast calf's liver with fresh herbs

For this dish you need a whole calf's liver, larded by the butcher 4 or 5 times lengthwise, and tied into the shape of a joint of beef, but not barded. A whole liver weighs 2–2.3 kg (4 lb 8 oz–5 lb 2½ oz) and will serve 10–12 people. It may be an expensive dish, but is amply justified by its great delicacy and the lack of waste—any leftovers can be eaten cold, and are still most presentable, as well as delicious. Order from your butcher well in advance and then you can be certain that the liver won't have been refrigerated or frozen.

For 10–12   1 whole calf's liver weighing 2–2.3 kg (4 lb 8 oz–5 lb 2½ oz)
1 bowl each of parsley, chervil and chives – one bowl should give about 200 ml (⅓ pint; ⅞ cup) chopped herbs
¼ bowl thyme
1 tablespoon rosemary
½ bowl mint
1 piece of pig's caul (from the butcher)
1 large, very thin, piece of barding fat
3 cloves of garlic
400 ml (⅔ pint; 1¾ cups) degreased bouillon
10 juniper berries
2 liqueur glasses good Cognac (Fine Champagne) or Armagnac
1 lemon
100 g (3½ oz; ½ cup) butter
salt, pepper

Chop all the herbs one after the other, and mix together. Wash the caul in warm water, lay it out on a board and pat dry. Sprinkle liberally with the herbs, but don't use them all, and season with salt and pepper. Roll it tightly round the liver, tying both ends with string like a parcel and trimming off any surplus caul. Then surround with the barding fat and secure with string.

Preheat the oven to 230°C/450°F/Mark 8. Put the meat in a large ovenproof dish with the whole garlic cloves, and colour rapidly all over for about 25 minutes. Then take the dish out of the oven, pour off the fat and pour in a bowl of the hot bouillon. Add all the rest of the herbs except half a bowl, the crushed juniper berries and 1 glass of the brandy. Return to the oven, turned down to 200°C/400°F/Mark 6, and cook for another 35 minutes, turning the meat twice. To test if it is done, insert a trussing needle right into the centre of the meat: the point should be very hot when you pull it out.

Take out the meat and keep it hot without allowing it to continue cooking. Deglaze the dish with the rest of the bouillon and the lemon juice, bring to the boil and then strain through a fine-meshed sieve or conical strainer into a saucepan. Bring to the boil again, add the rest of the herbs, turn off the heat, put the lid on and leave to infuse for 2–3 minutes. Then pour in the rest of the brandy, check the seasoning, and reheat. Off the heat, add the butter in pieces, whisking it in as it melts. Serve the liver carved into slices almost 1 cm (½in) thick, and hand round the sauce in a sauceboat. The ideal accompaniment would be wild rice, cooked according to the instructions on the packet.

Provençal caillettes

These are like small sausages of pork and pig's liver, wrapped in pig's caul, packed into a dish and cooked in the oven. They can be eaten hot or cold.

For 12 1 kg (2 lb 4 oz) pig's liver
caillettes 250 g (8¾ oz) boned pork chine
500 g (1 lb 2 oz) fresh fat bacon
2 whole pieces of pig's caul
6 cloves of garlic
12 tablespoons chopped parsley
2 teaspoons thyme leaves
1 bayleaf crumbled or powdered
salt, pepper

Ask your butcher to slice off the liver, chine and bacon 1 cm (½ in) thick, and at home cut into squares of 7–8 cm (3 in). Crush the garlic cloves and mix with the herbs. Put all in a dish, season with salt and pepper, mix and leave in a cool place for 4 hours for the flavours to blend.

Preheat the oven to 200°C/400°F/Mark 6. Wash the caul in warm salted water, and spread out carefully without tearing. Cut into squares of about 12 cm (5 in), and divide the ingredients between them, building them up in alternate layers. Fold over the edges of the caul to seal the packets, and shape into balls. As they are ready, place in an ovenproof dish, crowding them in quite tightly. Bake in the oven for 1 hour, watching that the surface does not brown, then lower the heat to 180°C/350°F/Mark 4 for the last 20–30 minutes. When served hot, accompany with chips and a highly seasoned green salad with tarragon; when cold, the salad on its own is enough.

Roast shoulder of mutton with vegetables

Homely, delicious and causing no anxiety to the cook, this dish is unique in all senses of the word. The shoulder of mutton is unboned, which brings out its best.

For 6 1 shoulder of young mutton with the bone
1 clove of garlic (optional)

butter or oil
1 kg (2 lb 4 oz) potatoes
1 teaspoon thyme
500 g (1 lb 2 oz) firm tomatoes
salt, pepper

Preheat the oven to 200°C/400°F/Mark 6. Insert slivers of garlic in the mutton, if used—but it's not essential. Smear the joint by hand with butter or oil seasoned with salt and pepper. Peel the potatoes and cut into cubes, not too large, as if for sautéeing. Slice the tomatoes into fairly thick rounds. Grease the roasting pan with a spoonful of oil, distribute the potatoes evenly over the base, season with a little salt and sprinkle over half the thyme. Cover with the tomato slices, and place the meat on top, resting on a metal grid.

Put in the oven, on the middle rung, and allow 20 minutes per 500 g (1 lb 2 oz), assuming that the meat started at room temperature. Half way through, turn the shoulder over, and sprinkle the contents of the roasting pan with the rest of the thyme. As it cooks, the juices and fat from the mutton will impregnate the potatoes, which are kept moist by the tomatoes.

Leg of mutton boulangère

For this dish, the leg of mutton is roasted on a bed of sliced, strongly seasoned and already cooked potatoes. The secret of success lies in the fact that the potatoes must be completely cooked when the meat is added.

1 whole boned leg of mutton weighing 1.5–2 kg (3 lb 6 oz–4 lb 8 oz)
1 heaped teaspoon thyme leaves
½ teaspoon marjoram leaves
2 bayleaves
3 sage leaves
6 coriander seeds
2 kg (4 lb 8 oz) potatoes
1 fine onion
2 cloves of garlic
100 g (3½ oz; ½ cup) butter
salt, pepper

Remove the meat from the refrigerator 4 hours in advance, to be sure that it cooks properly, and allow 1 hour 30 minutes for cooking the potatoes. Preheat the oven to 200°C/400°F/Mark 6. First, prepare the herbs, stripping the leaves off the thyme and marjoram, and crushing the bayleaves, sage and coriander seeds. Chop the onion finely. Peel the potatoes, slice into thin rounds and put in a dish with the herbs, 1 teaspoon salt, pepper from the mill and the onion. Squeeze over 1 clove of garlic with the garlic press, or grate it. Mix all together well with both hands, transfer to a long ovenproof dish and rub with the second garlic clove. Pour on enough hot water to come level with the top of the potatoes, and dot the surface with half the butter.

Put in the oven on the middle rung and, when the water is boiling and the top is beginning to dry out, cover the dish with a sheet of foil. Stir the potatoes around occasionally with a long-handled spoon and, when they have settled and are almost cooked, remove the foil and lower the heat to 180°C/350°F/Mark 4. Let them turn golden; they will be cooked when there is practically no water left in the bottom of the dish.

Weigh the leg of mutton to estimate the cooking time, at 15–18 minutes per 500 g (1 lb 2 oz). Work the rest of the butter together with ½ teaspoon salt and a good pinch of pepper, spread all over the meat and place on top of the potatoes. Turn up the oven to 220–230°C/425–450°F/Mark 7–8, and return the dish, positioning it one rung lower down. When the joint is coloured, turn it over and, at the end of the cooking time, turn off the oven and leave to rest for 5 minutes with the door half open. To serve, bring the dish to the table and carve the mutton on a board. Save the juices and add to the potatoes.

Stuffed leg of mutton with herbs

This dish consists of a boned leg of mutton, stuffed with fried lamb's kidneys and herbs, tied to reshape it and larded with a little garlic. It is carved like an ordinary joint and, if it is firmly tied, it can be spit-roasted.

For 6   1 leg of mutton weighing about 1.3 kg (2 lb 14½ oz)
                 3 lambs' kidneys
                 60 g (2 oz; ¼ cup) butter

2 teaspoons thyme and 1 teaspoon each savory and
  oregano
3 large basil leaves, chopped
a pinch of rosemary leaves
1 clove of garlic
salt, pepper

Ask your butcher to bone the leg of mutton, saving the main part of
the knuckle bone, which will be used to re-form the joint. Open the
kidneys without separating the lobes. Melt a large nut of butter with
1 tablespoon of the mixed herbs in a frying pan, then quickly seize the
kidneys over a moderate heat, and season with salt and pepper; don't
let them continue cooking, they should remain very pink inside.

Preheat the oven to 220°C/425°F/Mark 7, 15–20 minutes in advance.
Stuff the leg with the kidneys, opening them out and laying them
end to end, insert the knuckle bone as far as the fleshy muscle, and tie
with string to give the joint a regular shape. Lard with small slivers of
garlic, and weigh the meat to calculate the cooking time, allowing
18–20 minutes per 500 g (1 lb 2 oz). Add a pinch of the mixed herbs to
the cooking butter from the kidneys, season with salt and pepper, and
spread this over the leg. Place on a metal grid in a roasting pan, and
put in the oven, turning so that it colours on all sides. Then lower the
heat to 200°C/400°F/Mark 6 and baste with 1–2 tablespoons water.

When the cooking time is up, turn off the oven and leave the joint
to rest for 5 minutes with the door half open. Glaze the roasting pan
with 1 tablespoon boiling water, scraping up all the deposits with the
back of a fork. Bring to the boil and, off the heat, add the rest of the
butter, shaking the pan so that the sauce becomes shiny-smooth as it
melts. Taste and season with salt and pepper. Carve the leg of
mutton, and collect the juices to add to the sauce in the sauceboat.
Serve with a mixture of white haricot beans and French beans,
sprinkled with butter.

Pork civet

To bind the sauce of this stew you will need to ask your butcher for a
little pig's blood—that's the secret of the glistening, smooth sauce of a
civet. It should be made with meat from a young pig, although you
can use ordinary pork, in which case you should cook it for at least
2 hours to be sure that it is tender.

For 6   1.5 kg (3 lb 6 oz) chine, blade, or spareribs or pork
                 with fat removed
             150 g (5¼ oz) mild salt belly pork
             5 tablespoons pig's blood
             2 tablespoons lard, or goose or duck fat
             2 tablespoons flour
             1 bottle of good quality red wine
             1 bouquet garni with a sprig of hyssop
             6 medium onions
             1 clove of garlic
             4 sage leaves
             salt, pepper, nutmeg

Ask the butcher to bone the pork and cut it into chunks. Slice the salt belly into small sticks, and blanch for 5 minutes in boiling water. Then drain and wipe dry, colour slowly in a large heavy pan, take out and reserve. Add the lard or goose or duck fat to the fat in the pan, and put in the pieces of pork. As soon as they begin to brown, sprinkle with the flour, stir for a few minutes, and pour in the wine. Add a little water, if necessary, so that the meat is just covered with liquid. Bring to the boil, add the herbs, onions, garlic, salt, pepper and nutmeg, and cover the pan. Simmer over a low heat for 1 hour 30 minutes to 2 hours or more.

Ten minutes before serving, thin the pig's blood with a few spoonfuls of the hot sauce and, off the heat, pour into the pan, stirring all the time. Return to a very gentle heat for the blood to thicken the sauce, but don't let it boil which would curdle the liquid. Check the seasoning—it should be fairly strong. Serve with buttered pasta or boiled potatoes.

Pork chops with herbs

Whether you are using loin or sparerib chops, the cooking is the same. They are coated with herbs an hour in advance, then browned in the frying pan and finished in the oven. You can serve any vegetable with them, but white haricot beans, fresh or dried, with butter, parsley and a hint of garlic, go very well.

For 6   6 pork chops weighing about 180 g (6¼ oz) each
             dried mixed herbs

1 tablespoon lard
50 g (1¾ oz; ¼ cup) butter
salt, pepper

Season the chops with salt and pepper, and coat each side with a pinch of the herbs, pressing them in so that they stick. Leave in a cool place for 1 hour.

Preheat the oven to 200°C/400°F/Mark 6. Heat the lard in a frying pan, and lightly colour the chops, but don't worry about cooking them through. As they are done, place in an ovenproof serving dish, then cover with a sheet of foil, and bake in the oven for 10 minutes to finish cooking. Just before serving, dot with the butter. The subtlety of this dish rests in not overdoing the herbs.

Roast leg of pork with herbs

The pork leg should be the top part or thigh, taken from a young pig, fresh (that is, not salted) and still with the rind on.

For about 10   1 leg of pork weighing 2.5–3 kg (5 lb 10 oz–6 lb 12 oz)
1 teaspoon coriander seeds
2 heaped tablespoons mixed herbs
2 tablespoons lard
salt, pepper

Crush the coriander seeds in a mortar or peppermill. Make a thick paste with all the herbs and aromatics and the lard, seasoning fairly strongly with salt and pepper. Score the rind of the pork in squares of 2–3 cm (1 in), and insert some of the paste in the cracks. These will open up with the heat, and you will use up the rest of the paste to fill them during cooking. Weigh the joint, and place on the metal grid of a roasting pan in the cold oven. Then light the oven, set at 200°C/400°F/Mark 6, so that it heats up slowly and, from the moment when the pork begins to colour, calculate the cooking time at 25 minutes per 500 g (1 lb 2 oz). With this timing, the meat will come out rosy pink if it starts from room temperature, but if you take it straight from the refrigerator it will require a little longer.

If the oven heats up very quickly from the bottom, line the roasting pan with a large sheet of foil, and do not allow the juices to burn during cooking. Add a spoonful of water from time to time and, when the joint is a nice golden all over, having turned it, lower the temperature to 180°C/350°F/Mark 4 and cover with foil. At the end of the cooking time, test to see if the meat is done by plunging a trussing needle right into the centre; the point should be burning hot when you pull it out. Turn off the oven and leave the joint to rest for another 10 minutes.

To carve, strip off the rind with its layer of fat, and separate into squares. Serve these with slices of the pork, cut thin as for a leg of mutton. Deglaze the roasting pan with a little boiling water, scraping up the caramelized bits with the back of a fork. Pour off the fat, if necessary, and hand round in a sauceboat. There are many vegetables to choose from as an accompaniment: sautéed or puréed potatoes, fresh or dried haricot beans, cabbage, spinach.

Roast fillet of pork charcutière

In this recipe, the pork is first poached in water with herbs, then finished in the oven. This method results in tender, juicy meat, and the joint only loses about 10 per cent in weight, as opposed to 20 per cent or more in ordinary direct roasting. If you like to lard your pork roasts with slivers of garlic, you can do this in the normal way. The sage is added to the sauce and, as well as flavouring, it makes fatty meat more digestible. Roast pork is just as good cold as hot, so buy enough for two meals, allowing 200 g (7 oz) per person.

For 6   1.5 kg (3 lb 6 oz) boned fillet of pork, or 2 kg (4 lb 8 oz)
                with the bone
             2 carrots
             2 onions
             4 shallots
             4 cloves of garlic
             1 bouquet garni
             1 clove
             salt, 6 peppercorns
             6 sage leaves
             1 tablespoon butter

Weigh the joint. Slice the vegetables and put in a large heavy pan with all the herbs and seasonings except the sage. Cover with water, put the lid on and boil over a high heat for 15 minutes. Then add the pork and enough water to half cover it, put the lid on, and poach steadily for 15 minutes for each 500 g (1 lb 2 oz) for a joint of average thickness; add on a few more minutes if it is thicker. Turn half way through the cooking time.

Preheat the oven to the maximum temperature 15 minutes before the pork is ready. When it is done, add the crumbled sage leaves, turn off the heat and allow to rest for 5–8 minutes. Then take out the joint, place on the grid of the roasting pan, and put in the oven for about 20 minutes until golden all over. Meanwhile, pour off the fat from the poaching liquid, strain into a wide pan and reduce over a high heat to the equivalent of a large glassful. Carve the meat when it is ready, collecting the juices and adding them to the reduction, together with those from the roasting pan. Heat to boiling point and, off the heat, thicken to a smooth sauce with the butter, swirling it around by shaking the pan as it melts.

Blade of pork with sage

Blade of pork is part of the front shoulder, above the leg, and is a delicious cut. If you roast it with the bone in, it is more difficult to carve but has, so it is said, more flavour. If it is boned, it should be tied into a neat shape and, of course, it doesn't need any barding fat.

For 6   1 blade of pork weighing about 1.5 kg (3 lb 6 oz)
                20 small dried sage leaves
                100 g (3½ oz; ½ cup) lard
                2 medium onions
                1 clove of garlic
                2 shallots
                salt, pepper

Stud the pork all over with the sage, using 2 leaves at a time, stuck together with a little lard seasoned with salt and pepper, and buried well into the meat. Put 1 tablespoon of the lard into a heavy casserole, and lightly brown the joint and the onions, over a moderate heat so that the fat does not burn. When the pork is a beautiful golden colour, lower the heat, add 1–2 tablespoons cold water, the garlic and shallots, season lightly with salt and cover the pan. Cook at a gentle simmer, turning the joint once or twice and seasoning again with salt, very sparingly, and pepper from the mill. Allow 1 hour 45 minutes for a boned blade, 1 hour 30 minutes with the bone in.

When it is done, carve and serve in slices, with the cooking juices in a sauceboat, after pouring off any fat. Potatoes, carrots, lentils or puréed haricot beans would all be a good choice of vegetable; brussels sprouts, when available, also go very well, and, similarly, hearted cabbage and spinach.

Potée champenoise

French homely soups known as 'potées' were, for many centuries, the principal food of country districts, although the ingredients have been much augmented since their adoption by the towns. This version is from the province of Champagne, as the name indicates, and presides over the traditional banquet held at the end of the grape harvest. It is a meal in itself, but it was not always such a rich and sumptuous dish.

For about *8–10*	1 lightly salted pork hock or small ham 600 g (1 lb 5 oz) mild salt belly pork 1 corn-fed chicken weighing 2.5 kg (5 lb 10 oz) 6 carrots 2 onions 2 cloves 3 turnips 1 head of celery 12 medium potatoes 1 truffled Lyon 'saucisson', or large, lightly cured, pork poaching sausage 1 small Morteau 'saucisson', or smoked pork liver sausage 1 kg (2 lb 4 oz) fresh white haricot beans, shelled, or 400 g (14 oz) dried white haricot beans 1 bouquet garni salt, 10 peppercorns

If you are using dried haricot beans, soak them for 2 hours in warm water to swell. Rinse the salt pork, put into a large saucepan with 5 litres (8¾ pints; 11 US pints) cold water, bring to the boil and skim. When the liquid has cleared, lower the heat and cook at a gentle boil for 1 hour 30 minutes to 2 hours. Then add the carrots, the onions stuck with the cloves, the turnips, the heart of the celery, and the peppercorns. Meanwhile, truss the chicken as for roasting, so that it keeps its shape, and add 20 minutes later, along with the sausages. When the liquid has come back to the boil, allow 20 minutes per 500 g (1 lb 2 oz) at a gentle boil. Taste before seasoning with salt and, 30 minutes before the end of the cooking time, add the potatoes.

While the potée is cooking, prepare the haricot beans. If you are using fresh ones, cook them in boiling water, gently so that they do not burst, with the bouquet garni and a stick of celery. Season with salt when they are three-quarters done. The same principles apply if you are using dried beans, which should be started in at least 2 litres (3½ pints; 4½ US pints) cold water, but salted only at the end of the cooking time.

To serve, slice the meat and sausages, and arrange in a dish, with the vegetables separately. Accompany with the usual condiments—coarse salt, various types of mustard, gherkins, pickles, barbecue sauce (see p. 51), oil and vinegar.

Don't forget the cooking liquid from the potée and beans. Combine them, in the proportions that suit you, and add the heart of a loose-leafed cabbage, first blanched in boiling water and shredded. Cook for 30 minutes and you have a marvellous cabbage soup for another meal. Put some slices of crusty white bread in the bottom of a soup tureen, and pour over the piping hot soup.

Barbecued pork spareribs

Spareribs are taken from above the chops, with the fat removed. They can be roasted in the oven, or grilled on the barbecue after rubbing them with spiced salt and leaving them for 8–12 hours to absorb the flavours. They are painted with barbecue sauce during cooking. Serve with potatoes baked whole in foil, accompanied by butter, cream cheese lightened with cream and seasoned with salt, pepper and a mixture of herbs with chives predominating.

For 6   1.8 kg (4 lb) pork spareribs with fat removed

THE DRY MARINADE
500 g (1 lb 2 oz) coarse salt
1 tablespoon crushed white and black peppercorns
4 cloves
12 juniper berries
1 teaspoon quatre épices
1 tablespoon mixed dried thyme, bayleaf, oregano
    and rosemary

THE SAUCE
300 ml (½ pint; 1¼ cups) barbecue sauce (see p. 51)

THE GARNISH
6 good sized potatoes
250 ml (scant ½ pint; 1⅛ cups) fresh cream cheese
100 g (3½ oz; ⅜ cup) fresh cream
chives
125 g (4¼ oz; ½ cup) butter
salt, pepper

Ask the butcher to give you the spareribs whole (not cut up)—which will keep them moister during cooking—and completely free of fat. Crush the spices and mix them and the herbs with the salt. Rub all over the meat, place in a long earthenware or glass dish, cover with the rest of the spiced salt and leave to marinate.

To roast, preheat the oven to the maximum temperature 15–20 minutes in advance. Take the pork out of the dry marinade and wipe, but leave any herbs which may be clinging. Place the pieces flat in a roasting pan without overlapping, put into the oven on the middle rung, and sweat for 10–12 minutes to release the excess fat. Pour this off, then lower the heat to 200°C/400°F/Mark 6 and paint the spareribs liberally with the barbecue sauce, which you have thickened by reducing. Continue to cook for 45 minutes, basting frequently and adding a little water if the juices dry out. The sauce should glaze the meat, and brown without burning. When it is done, carve by simply cutting down between the bones, without dislodging the coating of sauce, and serve with the rest of the barbecue sauce, the potatoes and the garnish.

To barbecue, take the spareribs out of the spiced salt, wipe thoroughly and rub, if you like, with a little pressed garlic. Grill over the charcoal, paint the first side when it is cooked with the barbecue sauce, using a branch of savory or rosemary, and turn to cook the other side. Serve in the same way as for roast spareribs.

Grilled spiced steak

This preparation is at its best cooked over charcoal or, even better, over vine branches, and it's a choice dish for a barbecue party. If you use an infra-red oven grill, heat it to the maximum temperature 20–25 minutes in advance; and choose one thick slice of meat rather than two thin ones.

For 6   1.2–4 kg (2 lb 11 oz–3 lb 2 oz) upper fillet or rump steak of beef, in 1 or 2 slices depending on your type of grill
1 sliver of star anise
1 small hot pimento
1½ teaspoons thyme leaves
1 level teaspoon salt
1 level teaspoon crushed black and white peppercorns
60 g (2 oz; ¼ cup) butter

Crush the star anise and pimento and, 2 hours before cooking, put all the seasonings in a glass of boiling water, and leave for the flavours to infuse.

Heat the grill in advance until very hot. Just before cooking, pour the seasoned water into a large dish and soak the slices of meat for 3–4 minutes on each side. Drain and immediately put under the grill, cooking until very rare, rare or medium, according to taste, and keeping an eye on them. Have ready a hot serving dish in which the butter has just melted and, as soon as the steak is done, transfer it to the dish and turn the slices to coat them with the butter on both sides. Serve in the French style, with fried potatoes or chips, or in the American manner, with baked jacket potatoes and a bowl of cream mixed with green herbs.

Normandy-style grilled steak

This consists of a beautiful upper fillet, grilled and served on a bed of boiled or sautéed new potatoes. The Normandy touch is the plentiful use of chopped parsley, first steeped in seasoned cream for a couple of hours, then scattered over the meat and potatoes.

For 6   2 slices from the upper fillet of beef weighing
              400–500 g (14 oz–1 lb 2 oz) each
          1 generous teacup chopped parsley
          4 tablespoons thick fresh cream
          1.5 kg (3 lb 6 oz) small new potatoes
          80 g (2¾ oz; ⅜ cup) butter
          2 tablespoons oil
          salt, pepper

Season the cream lightly with salt and pepper, and macerate the parsley in it for 2 hours. Allow 45 minutes to 1 hour for the potatoes, depending on their size and age, and cook slowly in the butter and oil until they are golden and tender.

Fry or grill the steak, very rare, rare or medium according to taste, and season with salt and pepper as soon as you turn it over. To serve, drain the potatoes and spread over the bottom of a dish, seasoning with salt, lightly, and with pepper. Place the meat on top and cover the whole with the cream and parsley, heated without boiling. It is only by serving it in this way that you do justice to the delicacy of the dish, while the potatoes lightly coated with cream become a first-class vegetable.

Steak tartare

This is made with raw minced beef, mixed on the plate with herbs, capers, Worcester sauce, olive oil, bound with a raw egg yolk and seasoned with salt and pepper. Each plate is prepared in advance, and the guests then add their own flavourings and seasonings. Serve a fresh salad at the same time to add a finishing touch to an impressive cold dish.

For 6   900 g–1 kg (2 lb–2 lb 4 oz) finely minced steak
6 eggs
4 onions
6 teaspoons fines herbes (parsley, tarragon, chives, chervil)
125 g (4¼ oz) pickled capers
mustard, olive oil, Worcester sauce, tomato ketchup
2 lemons
salt, pepper

Tell your butcher what you want the steak for, and make sure that you get better quality than you would use for hamburgers, and more finely minced. Prepare each plate by shaping a round of raw mince in the centre. Separate the eggs and put the raw egg yolks in the half shells on top. Chop the onions and herbs apart, and drain the capers, which should be small ones. Distribute all these in small heaps around each plate. Cut the lemons in half.

Have the rest of the ingredients on the table with the remaining herbs in small bowls, so that the guests can help themselves. Everyone prepares their own steak, starting with the egg yolk, a dash of mustard, and the seasonings on their own plate, followed by the oil, a few drops of Worcester sauce, salt and pepper, mixing everything well with a fork, adjusting the seasoning to their own taste, and finishing up with the ketchup.

Tournedos with herb butter

Tournedos, or medallions of beef, are always cut fairly thick and taken from the smaller part of the fillet; they are surrounded with a thin bard of pork fat and tied. This is steak at its most succulent and delicate, cooked on or under the grill, or sautéed in butter in a frying pan over a brisk heat (the cooking juices are not used).

For 6   6 tournedos weighing about 180 g (6¼ oz) each
125 g (4¼ oz; ½ cup) butter
1 tablespoon chopped herbs, equal parts of parsley, chervil, chives
1 level teaspoon mustard
1 lemon
salt, pepper

First make the herb butter to give the flavours a chance to blend. Work the butter with a fork together with the herbs, mustard, salt, pepper and a few drops of lemon juice. Roll into a sausage-shape, wrap in foil and refrigerate.

Season the tournedos on both sides with salt and pepper 30 minutes before cooking. Assuming that they are about 2 fingers thick, allow 3½ minutes on each side for very rare, 5 minutes for rare, and 6 minutes for medium. Grill or sauté over a good heat, but not too high, so that the barding fat becomes transparent and golden round the edges. Arrange them in a hot serving dish, with a round of herb butter on each. Sautéed or puréed potatoes, gratin dauphinois (see p. 120), or French beans with butter all go well with tournedos, but the classic accompaniment is the delicate béarnaise sauce (see p. 52).

Veal escalopes with herbs

You can buy the butcher's ordinary veal escalopes to serve two or three people, but if you want to make a special dish for a larger number, ask him to cut you small escalopes of 60g (2oz) each, allowing two per person, and to trim them to a fairly even thickness and shape.

For 6   12 small escalopes weighing 60g (2oz) each
1 bunch of watercress
1 bunch of parsley
2 sprigs of tarragon
125g (4¼oz; ½ cup) cream
1 lemon
flour
100g (3½oz; ½ cup) butter
salt, pepper

Start by preparing the herbs. Pick off the leaves and tender stalks from half the watercress, and chop finely together with the parsley and tarragon; you should have 4 generous tablespoons of greenery. Mix with the cream, season with a pinch of salt and pepper, and add the juice of half the lemon by small spoonfuls, tasting as you go, to obtain a sharp but not acid flavour. Leave at room temperature for the flavours to mellow.

Preheat the oven to 200°C/400°F/Mark 6. Sprinkle a board with the flour, salt and pepper, dip in the escalopes and shake off the excess. Heat the butter in a frying pan, and lightly colour the escalopes over a moderate heat, without the butter browning—don't worry about cooking the meat right through. As each escalope is ready, place in an ovenproof serving dish and keep in the oven with the door open. Then pour the cream and herbs into the frying pan, and heat to boiling point over a fairly fast flame, scraping up the caramelized bits from the bottom of the pan. As soon as the cream is thick enough to coat the wooden spoon, add a few drops of lemon juice and pour over the escalopes. Put in the oven to heat through and finish cooking the veal, without letting it bubble. Garnish with the rest of the water-cress. A good choice of accompaniment would be seasonal green vegetables—French beans, peas or spinach—and sautéed new potatoes.

Grenadins of veal with green peppercorns

Veal grenadins look like beef tournedos, and appear as small rounds of the fillet encircled with a thin piece of barding fat. Sometimes the butcher will also cut them from the leg end of the fillet. Green peppercorns are sold frozen in small packets, or freeze-dried in jars. As for the cream, I would choose pouring cream (like whipping cream); but thick or double cream has its advocates.

For 6   6 veal grenadins weighing about 150–180 g
                    (5¼–6¼ oz) each
               flour
               100 g (3½ oz; ½ cup) butter
               1 liqueur glass Cognac
               200 ml (⅓ pint; ⅞ cup) dry white wine
               4 teaspoons green peppercorns
               250 g (8¾ oz; 1 cup) fresh cream
               1 teaspoon tomato concentrate
               salt

   Lightly flour the grenadins, just enough to dry the surface. Heat a good spoonful of butter in a frying pan, and lightly colour the veal over a very moderate heat, without allowing the butter to turn brown.

Take out the grenadins and put in a hot ovenproof serving dish. Sprinkle with the Cognac, cover and keep warm, allowing the flavours to blend. Deglaze the pan with the white wine, scraping up all the bits, and add the peppercorns, crushed in a mortar. Bring to the boil and reduce by half, then pour over the grenadins.

Put the cream into the frying pan with the tomato concentrate, and reduce until the cream has thickened and will coat the back of a spoon. Season with salt, pour onto the veal, and cook over a very gentle heat, uncovered, for 15–20 minutes, turning the meat once. As accompanying vegetables I would advise sautéed courgettes (squash) or cucumbers (see p. 116), or French beans, and, when available, boiled new potatoes.

Milanese osso-buco

A traditional Milanese stew, with its distinctive character derived from the 'gremolata'—a mixture of parsley, garlic and orange and lemon peel, added just before serving.

For 6

1.5–1.7 kg (3 lb 6 oz–3 lb 13 oz) knuckle of veal
250 g (8¾ oz) carrots
250 g (8¾ oz) onions
6 tomatoes
3 tablespoons olive oil
6 large basil leaves, or 2 teaspoons dried basil
1 celery stick
1 sprig of oregano
a pinch of thyme
4 sage leaves
flour
250 ml (scant ½ pint; 1⅛ cups) dry white wine
1 chicken stock cube
salt, pepper

THE GREMOLATA
1 tablespoon chopped parsley
1 clove of garlic
peel of 1 lemon and 1 orange

Ask your butcher to cut the veal knuckles into rounds about 2 cm (1 in) thick. Grate the carrots and onions, skin and de-seed the tomatoes and chop roughly. Take a large, heavy casserole, and over a gentle heat soften the onions and carrots together in 1 tablespoon olive oil. When they are beginning to colour, add the tomato flesh, the basil leaves cut with scissors, the celery, oregano, thyme and sage. Cover the pan and simmer.

Lightly flour the veal slices, and brown in the rest of the olive oil in a frying pan. As they are ready, transfer to the casserole where the vegetables are cooking. Pour off the burnt oil from the frying pan, and deglaze with the white wine, scraping up the sticky bits from the bottom. Add the stock cube, dissolved in just enough water, and pour into the casserole, adding a little more water, if necessary, to cover the meat. Bring to the boil, taste and season with salt and pepper. Put on the lid, lower the heat and simmer over a very moderate fire for 1 hour 15 minutes to 1 hour 30 minutes. Correct the seasoning if necessary.

Prepare the gremolata by mixing together the chopped parsley, crushed garlic clove, and grated lemon and orange peel. Add to the hot osso-buco 5 minutes before serving, take off the heat, cover and leave for the flavours to blend. Serve with pilaff rice.

Stuffed breast of veal

Ask the butcher to bone the breast of veal, and to make a pocket where you can insert the stuffing. Keep any trimmings of meat and add them to the farce, which is based on spinach or chard, briefly cooked in boiling salted water to keep it green.

For 6–8   1.5 kg (3 lb 6 oz) boned breast of veal

THE FARCE
1 calf's brain
300 g (10½ oz) boned neck of pork
250 g (8¾ oz) onions
2 cloves of garlic
500 g (1 lb 2 oz) cooked spinach or green part of chard
100 g (3½ oz) stale white bread
1 cup of milk
1 teaspoon thyme leaves
2 teaspoons marjoram leaves
2 tablespoons chopped parsley

2 bayleaves
salt, pepper, nutmeg
2 eggs
4–5 large cabbage leaves
3 hard-boiled eggs

THE COOKING
60 g (2 oz; ¼ cup) butter
2 carrots
2 onions
2 shallots
1–2 cloves of garlic
1 bouquet garni
500 ml (scant pint; 2¼ cups) dry white wine
salt, pepper

Blanch the calf's brain in simmering salted water for 6–8 minutes, then drain and open out to cool quickly and firm up. Cook the spinach or chard for a few minutes in boiling salted water, so that it remains green. Soak the bread in the milk until swollen, and squeeze dry. Finely chop the pork, the veal trimmings (if any), the onions, garlic, cooked spinach or chard, and bread, and cut the cooled brain into cubes. Chop the parsley and crumble the bayleaves. Mix all these prepared ingredients together, plus the thyme and marjoram, and season with salt, pepper and nutmeg. Taste—the mixture should not be bland—then bind with the raw eggs.

Blanch the cabbage leaves in boiling water, and remove the large central ribs without tearing the leaves. Spread them out on a board: they are designed as a wrapping for the farce, making it easier to insert in the breast of veal. Place half the farce on the cabbage leaves, arrange the hard-boiled eggs on top end to end, and cover with the rest of the farce. Enclose the stuffing by folding over the cabbage leaves; don't worry about making a neat parcel, but trim off any surplus leaves. Slide into the pocket of the veal breast, and sew together the opening with kitchen thread. Carefully form the breast into a long, even shape, making sure that it is not too full and there is no risk of it bursting. Tie it round with stringnto four places to prevent it breaking open.

To cook, slice the carrots irounds and put into a casserole with the butter, whole onions, shallots, garlic and bouquet garni. Add the veal and heat over a moderate flame, colouring lightly without allowing the butter to burn. Pour in the white wine and enough water to come three quarters of the way up the meat, season with salt and pepper, cover the pan and bring to the boil. Then turn down the heat and simmer for 1 hour 15 minutes to 1 hour 30 minutes, turning the veal half way through. It won't dry out if cooked too long. When it is done, allow the dish to rest a little with the lid on, to develop the flavours. Then transfer the meat to a serving dish and carve into slices. Reduce the sauce in the casserole, uncovered, by boiling over a high heat, and serve in a sauceboat together with the vegetables.

Sauté of veal with green herbs

For 6
1.2 kg (2 lb 11 oz) boned shoulder or end chops of veal
100 g (3½ oz; ½ cup) butter
4 tablespoons chopped parsley
1 tablespoon finely cut chives
1 tablespoon chervil leaves
1 tablespoon roughly chopped tarragon leaves
200 ml (⅓ pint; ⅞ cup) dry white wine
1 lemon
2 tablespoons cream
salt, pepper

Ask your butcher to cut the meat into cubes of about 4 cm (1½ in). Preheat the oven to 200°C/400°F/Mark 6. Season the meat lightly on all sides with salt and pepper. Melt the butter over a moderate heat in a casserole, and lightly fry the meat so that the pieces just turn white; they must not brown. Then add the prepared herbs, off the heat, mixing them in carefully. Cover the pan, put in the oven and cook for 1 hour, turning the meat once or twice. The herbs should not fry and, if necessary, lower the heat to 180°C/350°F/Mark 4 and leave the door half open for 5 minutes.

At the end of the cooking time, lift out the meat with a skimmer and keep hot in the oven, turned off and with the door open. Put the casserole over a high heat, pour in the white wine, and add the juice of half the lemon and the cream. Boil very fast for 5 minutes, scraping up the bits from the bottom, and pour over the meat. Serve with leaf spinach, or with courgettes (squash), sautéed or as a gratin.

Veal tendrons with carrots

Tendrons come from the ribs which are a continuation of the cutlet bones. They are succulent morsels, cheaper than the noble cuts of veal, and make delicious stews.

For 6 1.2–1.5 kg (2 lb 11 oz–3 lb 6 oz) veal tendrons
1 small calf's foot
2 tablespoons flour
2 tablespoons oil
1.5 kg (3 lb 6 oz) carrots
250 g (8¾ oz) onions
100 g (3½ oz; ½ cup) butter
1 clove of garlic
1 bouquet garni of parsley, thyme, bayleaf, plus 1
  celery stick
1 glass red wine
salt, pepper

Ask the butcher to bone the calf's foot and cut into pieces. Blanch for 10 minutes in boiling salted water, drain and pat dry. Trim the tendrons of any fat, and dip them in the flour, which has been seasoned with salt and pepper. Brown lightly in the oil in a frying pan, over a moderate heat so that the fat does not burn, drain and reserve. Slice the carrots and onions into rounds, and sweat gently without colouring in the butter in a casserole. Add the garlic and bouquet garni, followed by the tendrons and pieces of calf's foot. Pour off any fat from the frying pan, add the wine, and bring to the boil, scraping up the bits with the back of a fork. Turn into the casserole, add a glass of water, and simmer for about 1 hour 45 minutes to 2 hours.

Taste and correct the seasoning if necessary. To serve, discard the bouquet garni, and arrange the tendrons and calf's foot on a serving dish, surrounded by the carrots. Accompany with buttered leaf spinach, or fine noodles with butter.

Niçoise-style veal tendrons

The tendrons should be selected without too much fat. In this recipe you can substitute shin of veal: it is very good prepared in the same way.

For 6   1.2–1.5 kg (2 lb 11 oz–3 lb 6 oz) veal tendrons
flour
3 tablespoons olive oil
4 onions
1 sweet pepper
3 carrots
1 bouquet garni, with 1 celery stick and a sprig of oregano
200 ml (⅓ pint; ⅞ cup) dry white wine
125 g (4¼ oz) green olives
2 aubergines
3 tomatoes
1 tablespoon chopped parsley
1 clove of garlic
100 g (3½ oz) small black olives
50 g (1¾ oz; ¼ cup) butter
salt, pepper

Cut the tendrons into even pieces, flour them lightly, and colour them in a good spoonful of the oil in a frying pan. As they are ready, transfer to a casserole dish. Slice the onions thinly, and grate the carrots. Put the sweet pepper under the grill to skin it, remove the seeds and cut into strips. Soften all these vegetable, plus the bouquet garni, in the frying pan over a moderate heat and, as soon as they begin to brown, turn onto the meat. Pour on the wine, and season lightly with salt and with pepper. Simmer for 1 hour 15 minutes.

Stone the green olives, blanch them by plunging into boiling water for a few minutes, and add them to the tendrons at the end of the cooking time. Meanwhile, skin the aubergines and cut into dice. Fry lightly in the rest of the olive oil in the frying pan, so that they are golden but not brown. Then pour off any excess oil, season with salt and pepper, and sprinkle with the parsley chopped with the garlic clove. Add the black olives, and keep hot without continuing to cook.

At the same time, cut the tomatoes across in half and scoop out the seeds with a small spoon. Season with salt and pepper, and put in the oven, preheated to 200°C/400°F/Mark 6. Bake, but don't let them completely break up.

To serve, arrange the veal in a dish surrounded by the tomatoes, and top with a spoonful of the aubergines, distributing the rest around the dish. Bring the juices in the casserole to the boil and, off the fire, add the butter in pieces, shaking the pan as it melts and makes the sauce smooth and thick. Pour over the meat. This delicious preparation can make a whole meal, accompanied by fresh buttered noodles or leaf spinach.

Veal loaf

This pâté is made with good, but cheap, cuts of veal and pork. It is an economical dish, without waste, and equally good hot or cold.

For 6
750 g (1 lb 10½ oz) boned neck of veal
250 g (8¾ oz) boned neck of pork
6 tablespoons chopped onions
6 tablespoons chopped celery sticks
2 cloves of garlic
1 bayleaf
2 tablespoons olive oil
200 ml (⅓ pint; ⅞ cup) dry white wine
1 teacup stale white breadcrumbs
2 tablespoons butter
nutmeg
½ teaspoon thyme leaves
2 eggs
1 piece of pig's caul (from the butcher)
salt, pepper

Ask your butcher to mince the meat finely, or do it yourself. Chop the onions, celery, garlic and bayleaf, and soften in the oil without colouring. Pour on half the wine, bring to the boil and cook for 2 minutes, then add the breadcrumbs and butter, and leave for another 2 minutes for the bread to swell. Mix all with the minced meat, season with salt and pepper, a little grated nutmeg and the thyme, and add the whole eggs; the mixture should be tasty and fairly highly sea-soned. Knead together until smooth and well integrated, then roll into a large sausage-shape and wrap neatly in the caul, previously soaked in warm water. Place in a dish or casserole.

Preheat the oven to 170°C/325°F/Mark 3. Bake the loaf for 25 minutes, then moisten with the rest of the wine, turn up the oven to 180°C/350°F/Mark 4, and cook for another 15 minutes. Altern-atively, cook in the casserole on top of the stove. First, colour gently on all sides in 1 teaspoon oil for about 25 minutes, then pour on the rest of the wine, cover the pan, and simmer over a low heat for about 40 minutes. Serve hot with puréed or sautéed potatoes or chips, or cold with a green salad.

Poultry and
Game

Chicken curry

This excellent dish is a meal in itself, and is just as good in summer as in winter. It can be left to simmer unattended, and will perfume the whole house. It can be made in the same way with pork or veal.

For 6–8   1 corn-fed chicken weighing 2.5–3 kg (5 lb 10 oz—6 lb 12 oz)
300 g (10½ oz) onions
2 tablespoons olive oil
2 cartons of natural yoghourt
2 tablespoons Madras curry powder
a pinch of saffron pistils, or a measure of saffron powder
500 g (1 lb 2 oz) tomatoes
3 cloves of garlic
20 coriander seeds
powdered cummin, cayenne pepper
salt, pepper

ACCOMPANIMENTS
rice
1 bowl of natural yoghourt
1 small bunch of mint
100 g (3½ oz) sultanas
1 banana
1 jar of mango chutney, mild or strong
100 g (3½ oz) grated coconut

Finely chop the onions, and soften without colouring in the oil in a large pan, over a moderate heat. Joint the chicken into medium-sized pieces, not too large, and add to the pan off the heat. Whisk the yoghurt with the curry powder and saffron. Skin and de-seed the tomatoes, and add them to the yoghourt, together with the crushed garlic cloves, coriander seeds, salt and pepper. Stir into the pan, mixing well, and leave the chicken to marinate in this mixture for 1 hour.

Pour in enough water to cover the chicken pieces, bring slowly to the boil, cover the pan and simmer for about 1 hour 30 minutes, without letting the chicken disintegrate to a pulp. While there will be more than a little sauce, it should not be too copious. Taste and correct the seasoning, which should be strong but not aggressively so. Then add a good pinch of cummin powder and, if necessary, 1 teaspoon curry powder and a dash of cayenne. Keep hot without continuing to cook.

Serve with the accompaniments: plain rice, simply cooked in water and dried out well; bowls containing the yoghurt with chopped mint, the sultanas, soaked in water to swell and drained, the banana sliced into rounds, and the coconut; and the mango chutney, which the guests should add to their plates in small quantities.

Chicken livers on skewers

This makes a delicate entrée, or the main course for a light dinner. Serve on its own, with a vegetable or salad, or even with a fried cake of polenta.

For 6   500 g (1 lb 2 oz) trimmed chicken livers
50 g (1¾ oz; ¼ cup) butter
1 teaspoon thyme leaves
3–4 leaves of rubbed sage
a small pinch of hyssop
20 very thin slices of smoked bacon
salt, pepper

Melt the butter slowly in a frying pan with the herbs, and cook gently for a little so that the flavours blend. Then add the livers, and sauté briskly to seal the surface and firm them. Remove from the heat, allow to cool slightly, and season lightly with salt and with pepper.

Collect the livers together in small groups of the same size, wrap in the slices of bacon, and spear with the skewers. Heat the grill, and cook under it, turning them, until the bacon is coloured and they are cooked.

Chicken baked in salt

For this recipe, a large roasting chicken is cooked in a casserole, completely buried in salt—fine white cooking salt will not do—it must be coarse sea salt, grey if possible. The crust becomes so hard that it has to be cracked with a hammer; but the chicken which emerges is not only cooked to a turn, but moist, coloured all over, full of flavour—and not at all over-salty.

For 6   1 oven-ready roasting chicken weighing 1.8–2 kg
  (4 lb–4 lb 8 oz)
2–3 chicken livers
1 sprig of savory, thyme or tarragon
1 small bayleaf
salt, pepper
4–5 kg (9 lb–11 lb 4 oz) coarse sea salt

Preheat the oven to the maximum temperature. Stuff the cavity of the chicken with the livers, seasoned with salt and pepper, and the herbs, and truss as for roasting. Take a casserole large enough to hold the bird surrounded by a salt crust 4 cm (1½ in) thick, and line the inside completely with a sheet of tinfoil. Spread a layer of salt 4 cm (1½ in) thick in the bottom. place the chicken on top breast-side down (not on its back), and cover all over with salt, packing it in round the sides; it should be completely buried, without any gaps or holes. Do not put the lid on, but put straight in the oven and bake for exactly 1 hour 30 minutes.

To serve, turn out the casserole onto a board, and break open the block all round the top, to disclose the chicken on its back, golden brown and puffed up—an amazing sight. If it has to wait to be served, halt the cooking 10 minutes earlier, and leave the casserole in the oven with the door open.

Roast chicken with garlic

The bird is cooked in a chicken brick—a special casserole of unglazed earthernware, shaped like a chicken—which should be soaked in cold water for half an hour or more beforehand. The chicken is stuffed with small cubes of fried bread rubbed with garlic.

For 4–5   1 chicken weighing about 1.5 kg (3 lb 6 oz)
4–5 slices of white bread
olive oil
1 whole head of garlic
1 heaped teaspoon dried thyme leaves
salt, pepper
flour

First, prepare the croûtons for the stuffing. The slices of bread should be about 1 cm (½ in) thick, with the crusts removed. Fry them in olive oil until golden on both sides, then rub with garlic and cut into small cubes. Season the inside of the chicken with salt and pepper, stuff with the croûtons, and tie with string, drawing the legs together to close the opening as much as possible. Put the rest of the garlic cloves, unpeeled. in the casserole, scatter with the thyme, and sprinkle with 1 tablespoon olive oil. Place the chicken on top, on its back.

Make a soft flour-and-water paste about the size of an orange, put it on a board or table and, with the palm of your hand, roll it into strands a finger thick. Stick down round the rim of the casserole, letting it overlap on the outside, put on the lid, and press round the edges so that it is hermetically sealed by the paste. Place in the cold oven, turn it on at 230°C/450°F/Mark 8 and leave to cook for 2 hours. When you lift the lid off the casserole, you will find a beautiful golden chicken, swollen by the cooking and with a delicate scent.

Basque-style chicken

Chicken in the Basque style is a French regional recipe which has been variously interpreted, although the ingredients are always the same. It should be a tasty dish, not a humble stew swimming in liquid.

For 6
1 chicken weighing about 1.5 kg (3 lb 6 oz)
4 sweet peppers, 2 each of red and green
olive oil
5 tablespoons dry white wine
4 medium tomatoes
6 onions
4 cloves of garlic
1 bouquet garni with a sprig of hyssop
salt, pepper

Begin by skinning the peppers. Oil them very lightly, put under the grill, turning often, until the skin begins to wrinkle. Then wrap in a moist cloth, and the skin will come away easily. Cut into strips. Joint the chicken, and colour the pieces slowly in 2 tablespoons oil in a frying pan, if necessary in 2 or 3 stages. As they are ready, transfer to a casserole, then season with salt and pepper, and moisten with the white wine. Leave over a gentle heat to finish cooking.

Plunge the tomatoes into boiling water to skin them, de-seed them, and chop roughly. Slice the onions and peel the garlic cloves, and soften without colouring in olive oil in the frying pan. Then add the tomatoes, peppers and bouquet garni, and season with salt and pepper. When all are reduced almost to a cream, turn into the casserole, and keep over a low heat until ready to serve, about 20–30 minutes.

Tarragon chicken

There are many ways of preparing tarragon chicken, but this is one of the better ones.

For 6	1 corn-fed chicken weighing about 2 kg (4 lb 8 oz)
	1 bunch of tarragon
	2 tablespoons oil
	100 g (3½ oz; ½ cup) butter
	1 carrot
	4 shallots
	4 medium white onions
	a pinch of thyme leaves
	1 liqueur glass of Cognac (optional)
	5 tablespoons dry white wine
	175 g (6 oz; ¾ cup) fresh cream
	1 egg yolk
	1 small bunch of chervil
	salt, pepper

Start by inserting 3–4 sprigs of tarragon, sprinkled with fine salt, into the cavity of the chicken; even if the poulterer has tied the bird, there should still be enough of a gap to do this. Heat the oil and 1 tablespoon of the butter in a large heavy pan, and put in the chicken, trussed as for roasting. Colour gently on all sides for 20–25 minutes, without letting the fat brown, then take out and keep hot. Grate the carrot, and slice the shallots and onions, and add to the pan with the thyme. Soften for a few minutes, stirring frequently, return the chicken, and sprinkle with the Cognac as soon as it has heated through. Moisten with the white wine and half its volume of water, add 2 whole sprigs of tarragon, and bring to the boil. Season with salt and pepper, cover the pan, and allow to simmer over a gentle heat for 30–40 minutes.

Remove the chicken to a serving dish, carve it, cover with a sheet of foil, and keep hot in the oven with the door open. Add the carving juices to the pan, and pour off the fat if necessary. Take out the tarragon, turn the contents of the pan into the liquidizer and reduce to a cream. Return to the pan, bring to the boil and, if there is too much sauce, reduce a little over the heat. Remove from the heat, add the cream beaten with the egg yolk. Taste and correct the seasoning, then add the leaves from the rest of the tarragon, the chervil cut with scissors, and reheat, stirring without letting it boil. Garnish the chicken with a few spoonfuls of the sauce, and hand round the remainder in a sauceboat. The most attractive vegetable accompaniment is small potatoes, fried in half oil, half butter, or goose fat, and drained well before serving.

Indian-style chicken

This is a meal in itself for any occasion. At first sight the long list of spices makes this dish look very complicated, but in fact it's no trouble to cook—and what a scent to greet you when you take the lid off at the table!

For 6–8   1 roasting chicken weighing 1.5–1.8 kg (3 lb 6 oz–4 lb)
1 lemon
2 150 g (5 oz) cartons of natural yoghourt
4 cloves of garlic
60 g (2 oz) fresh ginger, or 4 tablespoons powdered
   ginger
10 fresh mint leaves, or 1 dessertspoon dried rubbed
   mint
6 cloves
1 tablespoon coriander seeds
3 small hot pimentos
1 tablespoon cummin seeds
a good pinch of powdered cinnamon
2 large onions
1 wine glass olive oil
a pinch of saffron pistils
200 g (7 oz) rice
salt

Joint the chicken. Brush the skin of the lemon with warm soapy water (it will have been treated with chemicals) rinse, and grate the peel. Crush the garlic cloves. Put the chicken pieces in an earthenware dish with all the ingredients down to and including the cinnamon, mix, and leave to macerate for 30–45 minutes.

Meanwhile, take a thick-bottomed heavy pan in which the contents of the earthenware dish will be cooked, and heat the olive oil in it. Finely chop the onions, and soften over a very moderate heat for at least 20 minutes, stirring often. Then add the chicken with the contents of the dish, bring slowly to the boil, cover the pan and simmer for 20–25 minutes.

In a separate pan, bring to the boil 1 litre (1¾ pints; 4½ cups) salted water, with the saffron. Pour the rice in a shower onto the chicken, distributing it all over, add three quarters of the saffron water, and bring to the boil over a high heat. Maintain at a boil for 10 minutes, then lower the heat, cover the pan, and simmer gently for 45 minutes, without stirring. The rice should then have absorbed all the water. However, if the top is still not cooked, do not stir it, but gradually add the rest of the saffron water, which you have kept boiling in its pan, until the rice is perfectly cooked. Take off the lid and, still over a low heat, wait until the surface of the rice is pierced with lots of little holes. Serve the dish straight from the pan, with the beautiful golden rice, stirring just before.

You can have on the table bowls of sliced banana, quartered apple, chunks of pineapple, and almonds or peanuts, to soothe sensitive palates—served like the accompaniments to curries. Chutney, of mangoes or any other fruit, also gives a special touch.

Barbecued chicken

This is the sort of dish you eat with your fingers in the garden, nibbling celery sticks and potato crisps at the same time. Try with it some saucers of cummin powder, seasoned with salt; this is the spice of the North African barbecue, or 'méchoui', which everyone there sprinkles lightly on their meat.

For 6   3 small young chickens (or, better, 4)
4 tablespoons olive oil
1 teaspoon lemon juice
a pinch of dried thyme, oregano or savory
coriander seeds, powdered cummin
salt, pepper

First, prepare the marinade by mixing the oil, lemon juice and seasonings together. Split the chickens in half lengthwise, using scissors or a knife, since the bones should be quite soft. Remove the backbone and wishbone, and the small bones at the side. Brush the sides with the marinade mixture, and reserve in a covered dish for 20–30 minutes before cooking.

Heat up the barbecue until the charcoal is glowing and beginning to be covered with a fine white dust. Place the chicken halves on the grid, skin-side up, grill for 8–10 minutes according to size, and turn over. After 10–12 minutes, they should be cooked. Serve immediately.

American-style marinated chicken

For this preparation, the chicken pieces are smeared with a highly seasoned marinade, and left in a covered dish, turning occasionally, in the refrigerator where they will keep for at least a week. It is an ideal dish to eat alone as you can just take out a chicken portion without disturbing the others, and cook as required—frying, grilling or on the barbecue. For a barbecue party, serve it with grilled sweetcorn, or jacket potatoes with cream cheese and herbs.

For 6   2 young chickens weighing 1-1.2 kg (2 lb 4 oz–2 lb 11 oz) each
2 level tablespoons Meaux-type mustard (with small black seeds)
250 ml (scant ½ pint; 1⅛ cups) groundnut, corn or olive oil (according to choice)
2-3 cloves of garlic
a pinch of cayenne pepper
1 teaspoon thyme leaves
1 small bayleaf
1 teaspoon crushed black and white peppercorns
salt
2 tablespoons vinegar
2 tablespoons white wine

Joint the chickens into 4 pieces each, and remove the bones on either side of the vertebral column and from the breast. In a large bowl, work the mustard with the oil, pouring it in a thin stream as for a mayonnaise. Add all the herbs and spices one after the other, squeezing the garlic in a press and crumbling the bayleaf, to make a very shiny and highly seasoned sauce; from time to time add a drop of vinegar, alternating with the white wine. Paint each chicken portion generously with the mixture, place in a plastic container with a lid, and refrigerate for at least 24 hours (and up to a week).

If you are not outside using the barbecue, you can grill the chicken in the house. Place the pieces skin-side down on the grid of the grill pan and, when they are golden, turn to cook the other side.

Quick chicken

The young chickens are completely jointed, and are ready for the table after 25–30 minutes baking in the oven. They are served with a bowl of chopped parsley, just heated through in melted butter, and potato crisps. The carcases can be used to make a very good vegetable soup (see p. 77).

For 6   2 chickens weighing 1-1.2 kg (2 lb 4 oz–2 lb 11 oz) each
15–20 slices of smoked streaky bacon
salt, pepper
1 large bunch of parsley
150 g (5¼ oz; ⅝ cup) butter
a sliver of garlic (optional)

Preheat the oven to the maximum temperature. Joint and carve up the chicken as if it were cooked. Arrange the pieces in a single layer in a roasting pan, alternating with the slices of bacon, and season with salt and pepper. Put in the oven and, as soon as the surface is golden, turn over. The total cooking time will be scarcely more than 25 minutes.

Transfer to a serving dish, and accompany with a bowl of just melted butter, with the chopped parsley mixed in and a little squeezed garlic, if desired.

Roast duckling

This calls for young spring duckling, weighing scarcely 1 kg (2 lb 4 oz). They are cooked in the oven so that the skin becomes crisp and, with the first peas or tiny turnips of the season, they make a beautiful dish, which should be prepared with meticulous care.

For 4   2 duckling weighing 900 g–1 kg (2 lb–2 lb 4 oz) each
60 g (2 oz; ¼ cup) butter
1 lemon (optional)
salt, pepper

Preheat the oven to 200°C/400°F/Mark 6. Season the duck livers with salt and pepper, and put inside each bird with a small cube of butter about the size of a sugar lump. Sew up the openings; this is good practice with any roasting fowl, since it prevents the internal juices evaporating, and these can be added to the gravy after carving, and keep the flesh moist. Smear the skin by hand with some of the butter, place the duckling on their backs in a dish into which they will fit easily, but not with room to spare, and season with salt and pepper.

Put in the hot oven and, as soon as the breast is a light golden colour, after about 15 minutes, turn the birds onto their sides, and baste each one with 2 tablespoons hot water. About 15 minutes later, turn on to the other side and repeat. Allow a total cooking time of 40–45 minutes. Then take the dish out of the oven, cover with a sheet of foil and set aside for 5 minutes for the birds to rest. Lift them out while you pour off all the fat from the dish, return to the hot dish and carve each into four, collecting all the juices. Arrange the portions on a hot serving dish, cover with foil, and reserve in the still hot oven with the door open until ready to serve.

Add a little boiling water by the spoonful to the cooking juices in the dish, scraping up the deposit from the bottom with the back of a fork. Add a few drops of lemon juice, if used, bring to the boil, and add the rest of the butter in pieces, shaking the dish to make a smooth sauce. Just before serving, sprinkle the duck pieces with a few spoonfuls of sauce to glaze, and hand round the rest in a sauceboat, heated in advance. Serve your chosen vegetable at the same time. Glazed turnips (see p. 123), so delicate in springtime, are a particular favourite with duck.

Magrets

Ten years ago, magrets were almost unheard of, and very few people could have told you that they are the breast fillets taken from young adult ducks. They have since become fashionable, and have been adapted to various methods of preparation. In their native country, the Landes and Languedoc, magrets are simply grilled over vine branches; they are the greatest treat with potatoes sautéed in goose fat and topped with a slice of truffle, when available (Sarlat-style potatoes, see p. 121).In Paris, the poulterers sell magrets ready-prepared, and they are cooked in the frying pan like a steak—very rare, rare or medium. It is a subtle, luxurious dish, but easy.

For 6   4–6 duck magrets
              goose fat (if necessary)
              salt, pepper

Ask the poulterer for magrets with the skin on, and get him to cut off strips of skin lengthwise and give them to you at the same time. These can be served as a trimming, and, if the fillets are thin-skinned, they can also be used instead of the goose fat to grease the pan for cooking the duck.

Heat the frying pan until very hot, put in the magrets skin-side down and, when this side is golden, turn over and season with salt and pepper. Continue to cook to the degree desired, and be careful that the fat does not burn over too high a heat: people generally prefer their magrets rare or medium, and it is important not to overcook them. Lift out the duck and keep hot, pour off most of the fat from the pan (reserving it for another occasion), and scrape up the bits from the bottom of the pan with the back of a fork and 1 tablespoon hot water. To serve, slice the magrets in half with an oblique cut across—the juices which are released should be more or less pink, depending on the degree of cooking—and pour over them the boiling hot liquid from the pan.

Civet of goose

A civet always includes the blood of the bird (or animal) as a liaison or thickening for the sauce. For this reason you can be certain that this feast of a dish is at its very best when prepared in the country. If you cannot obtain goose blood, you can substitute pig's blood—an amount equivalent to a small carton of yoghourt—which you should order from the butcher. Duck, chicken and rabbit can be cooked in the same way.

For 8–10   1 young goose weighing 2.5–3 kg (5 lb 10 oz–6 lb 12 oz)
              3 level tablespoons flour
              1 bottle of red wine, preferably Mâcon
              3 onions
              4 shallots
              1 clove of garlic
              1 bouquet garni
              1 clove (optional)
              5 tablespoons goose or pig's blood
              salt, pepper

Ask your poulterer to joint the goose and cut into pieces. Reserve the gizzard and the liver with its fat. In a frying pan without fat lightly fry the pieces of goose so that they are scarcely coloured, starting with the fattest bits. As they are ready, drain and transfer to a casserole. When all are done, pour off the fat from the frying pan into a container, to reserve with any other fat from the bird for cooking; don't let it burn if you want to use it again. Thoroughly reheat the goose pieces in the casserole, sprinkle with the flour, and let it brown. Then pour in the wine, add enough water to cover and the onions, shallots, garlic, bouquet garni, clove (if used) and gizzard. Season with salt and pepper, put the lid on, and simmer for 1 hour 15 minutes.

Test to see if the goose is cooked: the meat should be tender but not disintegrating, and should come away easily from the bones if you encourage it, but not of its own accord. Remove the bouquet garni 10 minutes before serving, and add the whole liver, after trimming of excess fat with a spoon. Taste and correct the seasoning, and boil for another 5 minutes, to cook the liver. Thin the blood, which should not be coagulated, by mixing with a few spoonfuls of the sauce and, off the heat, add slowly to the casserole, stirring into the hot liquid. When it is completely incorporated, return to a very low heat for 5–10 minutes, being careful that it does not boil. The sauce should now be smooth, dark brown, glistening and velvety. Serve with buttered pasta or boiled potatoes. If necessary, the dish can be reheated over a very gentle heat without losing flavour.

Pheasant with sauerkraut

This recipe assumes that the pheasants are young roasting birds. They are not actually cooked with the sauerkraut, and so they preserve all their flavour and firmness. However, if you are supplied with an old cock pheasant more suitable for stewing, you can precook it in the way described, and then bury it in the casserole of sauerkraut, together with the cooking juices, to finish cooking. The same method can be applied to partridges, or even guinea fowl. There is no longer any need to sing the praises of sauerkraut: it is balm to the intestines, encouraging the production of lactic acid, and rich in vitamins, particularly sulphur. And, when served with dishes other than the rich pork which it often accompanies, it goes down well!

For 6–8   THE SAUERKRAUT
2 kg (4 lb 8 oz) uncooked sauerkraut
2 carrots
2 onions
2–3 tablespoons goose fat or lard
200 g (7 oz) pork rind without fat
1 tablespoon juniper berries
1 teaspoon cummin seeds
2 cloves
10 peppercorns
1 bottle Alsatian wine, preferably Riesling
800 g (1 lb 12¼ oz) smoked streaky bacon

THE PHEASANTS
2 pheasants
barding fat
125 g (4¼ oz) fat salt pork
6 sage leaves

1 onion
1 carrot
1 bouquet garni
1 small glass of Cognac (optional)
salt, pepper

Start with the sauerkraut which will need at least 2 hours and 30 minutes of cooking. Wash it in cold water, drain thoroughly and disentangle. Slice one of the onions and cut the carrots in 4 lengthwise. Put them in a large heavy pan with the goose fat or lard, and the trimmings from the pheasants—wings, neck and head. Colour without browning for a few minutes, then add the sauerkraut, and stir over a brisk heat until the excess moisture has evaporated. Put the pork rind into the bottom of the pan. fat side down, add the seasonings and the other onion, stuck with the cloves, and pour on the wine, which should just cover the ingredients. Put the lid on the pan, and now blanch the bacon for 20 minutes in boiling unsalted water, before adding to the sauerkraut. When it has returned to the boil, lower the heat and simmer.

The pheasants should be plucked, cleaned and singed, trussed and barded with the fat. If the poulterer prepares them for you, don't forget to ask for the trimmings, which go into the sauerkraut, and for the livers. Finely mince the fat pork to obtain a paste, season with salt and pepper, add the rubbed sage leaves, combine with the pheasant livers, and fill the cavity of each bird with the mixture. Slice the onion and carrot.

Preheat the oven to 200°C/400°F/Mark 6. Slowly colour the pheasants in a very little fat in a casserole, add the onion and carrot and bouquet garni, and sprinkle with the Cognac (if used).Put in the oven without a lid, and cook for about 35 minutes, turning them, and covering if they show signs of drying out. At the end of the cooking time they should be puffed up and shining.

Untruss the birds and remove the barding fat. Carve them, and collect the stuffing to add to the strained cooking juices. Discard the rind, trimmings and vegetables from the sauerkraut, and transfer to a serving dish with the carved pheasant on top. The sauce can be poured over or handed round in a sauceboat.

Pigeons with savory

For 6   6 small pigeons, or 3 large
                 125 g (4¼ oz; ½ cup) butter
                 1 tablespoon chopped savory
                 6 sage leaves
                 a pinch of thyme
                 1 clove of garlic
                 salt, pepper

Work together some of the butter with the savory, sage and thyme, and season with salt and pepper. Then put a large or small nut inside each pigeon, depending on the size of the birds. and tie with string to keep their shape.

Melt the rest of the butter in a heavy pan, large enough to hold the pigeons in a single layer, and colour them gently on all sides, without letting the butter burn. When they are golden, add 2 tablespoons cold water and the unpeeled garlic clove, cover the pan and braise over a very low heat for 45 minutes to 1 hour.

Transfer the pigeons to a serving dish, keeping the small ones whole or splitting the large ones lengthwise in half. Take out the garlic, and pour off the fat from the sauce if necessary. Alternatively, if the liquid is too much reduced, deglaze by adding a spoonful of boiling water, and scrape up the bits from the bottom of the pan with the back of a fork.

Stuffed rabbit

Perhaps garnished rabbit would be a better description: the somewhat unusual stuffing consists of various ingredients, chunky rather than smooth, and can make an original dish in its own right. Rabbit needs to be well flavoured and seasoned, and here it has a perfect complement.

For 6   1 young rabbit weighing about 1.5 kg (3 lb 6 oz)
                 200 g (7 oz) smoked streaky bacon
                 2 chipolata sausages
                 2 chicken livers
                 6 cloves of garlic

6 small onions
150 g (5¼ oz) button mushrooms
15 green olives
a large pinch of thyme
a pinch of marjoram
1 bayleaf
2 tablespoons olive oil
5 tablespoons dry white wine
1 bouquet garni
30 g (1 oz; ⅛ cup) butter
salt, pepper

Have the rabbit skinned and gutted, and keep the liver. Slice the bacon into small sticks, blanch in boiling water for 5 minutes, drain and wipe dry. Cut the chipolatas into pieces about 2 cm (1 in) long, divide the chicken and rabbit livers, and peel the garlic and onions. Cut the mushrooms, which should be small, not into strips but into quarters. Stone the olives, and blanch in boiling water for 5 minutes.

Colour the bacon slowly in a frying pan, lift out with a skimmer, and reserve in a dish. In the bacon fat, quickly sauté the chipolatas, livers, garlic and onions and, with the skimmer, transfer to the dish of bacon. Then add the mushrooms to the pan, and cook until they have given off their moisture. Combine all these ingredients, season with pepper and, lightly, with salt, and add the olives, thyme and marjoram, and crumbled bayleaf. Stuff the interior of the rabbit with the mixture, and sew up the skin.

Take a casserole large enough to hold the rabbit when curled round, and heat the oil in it. Colour the rabbit on both sides, add the white wine and bouquet garni, cover the pan, and simmer over a gentle heat for 1 hour to 1 hour 30 minutes or more, according to the size of the rabbit. When it is cooked, cut up the rabbit and re-shape it, with the stuffing spread out between the legs. Thicken the sauce with the butter, shaking the pan so that it melts, and hand round in a sauceboat.

Rabbit with prunes

In this dish, a young rabbit is braised with prunes, and dry Madeira gives the sauce a flavour which goes very well with the rabbit. The best prunes are those of Agen, in south-western France, noted for their thin skin and delicate taste.

For 6   1 young rabbit weighing 1.3–1.5 kg (2 lb 14½ oz–3 lb
    6 oz)
   12–15 prunes
   200 ml (⅓ pint; ⅞ cup) dry Madeira
   150 g (5¼ oz) cooked ham
   2 carrots
   2 onions
   1 tablespoon oil
   60 g (2 oz; ¼ cup) butter
   a pinch of dried thyme
   salt, pepper

Choose prunes which are vacuum-packed for preservation: they will be less dry. Stone them with a pointed knife, and leave them to macerate in the Madeira. Have the rabbit skinned and gutted, and ask for it to be cut up. Buy the ham in one thick slice, leave the fat on, and cut into dice. Slice the carrots and onions.

Put the oil and 1 tablespoon butter into a large heavy pan and, when it is hot, add the pieces of rabbit and colour slowly on all sides over a moderate heat. Five minutes before this process is finished, put in the ham, giving it just enough time to firm up, and the carrots and onions. Season with salt and pepper, and sprinkle in the thyme. Then pour on the Madeira from the prunes, together with 3–4 tablespoons water, distribute the prunes over the surface, cover the pan, and cook over a very low heat for 45 minutes, without stirring. Test to see if the meat is done—it might need a little longer depending on the age of the rabbit.

To serve, arrange the rabbit pieces in a hot serving dish, and garnish with the prunes. Heat the sauce until on the point of boiling and, off the heat, add the rest of the butter in bits, whisking it in for a smooth sauce. Pour over the rabbit. Fresh buttered noodles make an excellent accompaniment.

Sauté of rabbit with snail butter

For 4 1 rabbit weighing about 1.2 kg (2 lb 11 oz)
1 tablespoon groundnut oil
1 generous tablespoon butter
salt, pepper
about 250 g (8¾ oz) snail butter (see p. 60)

Prepare the snail butter the day before required. Roll into a sausage shape, wrap in foil and keep in a cool place, allowing all the flavours to blend and develop.

Have the rabbit skinned and gutted, and cut into pieces. Heat the oil and butter without colouring in a thick-bottomed frying pan, and lightly colour the rabbit pieces over a very moderate heat, still without letting the fat darken. This is a delicate operation, and you must watch the cooking carefully. If browning does start, you should add 1–2 spoonfuls of cold water immediately, turn the heat down to the minimum, and put the lid on the pan until the rabbit is cooked.

Turn up the heat slightly 5 minutes before serving, and add the snail butter in pieces so that it melts quickly, tossing the pieces of rabbit until they are all coated. It may not be necessary to use up all the butter, and you will have to judge. Taste and correct the seasoning, turn off the heat and cover the pan. Serve a few minutes later. Some of the best vegetables to go with it are potatoes, fried, boiled or steamed, and courgettes (squash), sautéed in oil.

Rabbit with tapénade

The rabbit is painted with tapénade—a delicious sauce—wrapped in pig's caul and baked in the oven. To make it easier to cut up at the end, ask your supplier to break the backbone, without separating the rabbit into pieces. The same recipe can be adapted for rabbit with mustard, smearing the animal with the mustard in the same way as the tapénade, but deglazing the pan with cream—100 g (3½ oz; ⅜ cup)—and bringing to the boil to thicken the sauce.

For 4   1 young rabbit weighing about 1.2 kg (2 lb 11 oz)
             1 piece of pig's caul (from the butcher)
             5 tablespoons or about 180 g (6¼ oz; ¾ cup)
                tapénade (see p. 62)
             200 ml (⅓ pint; ⅞ cup) dry white wine
             salt

Have the rabbit skinned and gutted. Detach the front legs and forequarters, reserving them, and also the breast, so that you have just the saddle left. Wash the caul in warm salted water, and stretch out on a board without breaking it. Generously paint the tapénade all over the inside and outside of the saddle, and coat the legs and forequarters as well, inserting these in the skin of the belly. Wrap the whole saddle in the caul, tie with string in 3 or 4 places including the ends, and pare away any surplus at the ends. Lay it out in a long ovenproof dish or just in a roasting pan.

Preheat the oven to 220°C/425°F/Mark 7. Put in the rabbit and, as soon as it begins to turn golden, moisten with the heated wine. Turn so that it is coloured all over, then lower the heat to 180°C/350°F/Mark 4. It should cook for 45 minutes to 1 hour, without drying out. Baste occasionally.

Transfer the rabbit to a serving dish and cut up. Pour off any fat from the cooking juices, add 1–2 tablespoons very hot water, scraping up the bits from the bottom of the pan, and pour over the rabbit. Serve with buttered pasta, French beans or sauté potatoes.

Fancies, Sweets and Pastries

Cervelle de canut

This recipe is a speciality of Lyon and despite its name—literally 'silk-weaver's brain'—it is not at all mysterious. The 'canuts' of Lyon were, and still are, craftsmen weavers of the finest silks in France. The preparation calls for cream cheese made from full cream milk, liberally flavoured with chopped herbs, which bring to the dish all their stimulating and digestive qualities.

> 500 g (1 lb 2 oz) drained cream cheese
> fresh herbs according to the season—chives, chervil,
>   parsley, tarragon, dill etc.
> 1 clove of garlic
> 125 g (4¼ oz) fresh cream
> vinegar
> 1–2 teaspoons oil
> salt, pepper

Choose a cheese which is sufficiently drained so as not to be too soft. Beat until smooth, finely chop the herbs, and incorporate them by the spoonful, stopping when they have been thoroughly absorbed by the cheese and are scarcely visible any more. At the same time, squeeze in a few drops, no more, of garlic with the garlic press.

The cheese is now ready for serving. However, perfectionists crown it by adding a few spoonfuls of cream, a dash of vinegar and a little oil. Stir to obtain the right consistency; it should be soft but not liquid. Serve cold with warmed slices of bread.

Goat's milk cheese in oil

For this preparation you need small goat's milk cheeses, scarcely dried. These are placed in a glass jar, large or small depending on the number of cheeses—the cheese should be generously covered with oil. Glass preserving jars with a hermetic seal are the best, and allow you to replace the cheeses as they are eaten. All fresh goat's milk cheeses can be treated in the same way, as long as they are sufficiently firm in texture not to disintegrate in the oil. The oil itself can be strained when it becomes too cloudy, and used in winter salads, to which it will add an exceptional flavour.

> 6 small goat's milk cheeses
> a small sprig of savory
> a branch of rosemary
> 1 hot red pepper, or 3 small hot pimentos
> 20 juniper berries
> 4 sprigs of dried fennel
> 1 bunch of thyme (5 sprigs)
> 2–3 cloves of garlic
> 1 dried bayleaf
> 1 litre (1¾ pints; 4½ cups) olive oil
> salt

Wash the cheeses between your hands in salted water, simply to clean and purify the skin. Put in a jar with all the herbs and seasonings, and the garlic cloves, unpeeled but crushed. Cover liberally with the olive oil.

After 48 hours, remove the rosemary and taste your cheeses, which should have a very delicate flavour. As you consume the cheeses, you can top up the jar with new ones.

Peaches trimmed with mint

For the sake of the appearance of the dish, choose white peaches, sound and ripe, if available, although yellow ones do just as well. The peeled peaches are arranged in each dish, and encircled with a light egg custard, flavoured with raspberries and a few rubbed leaves of mint, which intensify the tang; the inclusion of mint justifies the final touch—a sprig of two or three mint leaves in each fruit.

For 6
> 6 ripe peaches
> 500 ml (scant pint; 2¼ cups) whipping cream or 250 g (8¾ oz; 1 cup) thick cream
> 12 sugar lumps
> 6 yolks of egg
> 200 g (7 oz) raspberries
> a bunch of fresh mint

Wash the peaches carefully and place in a saucepan where they will fit comfortably without crowding. Pour on boiling water to cover, put the lid on, and allow to cook. Then peel them; the skin will come away very easily without damaging the fruit.

To make the custard, put the cream into a saucepan, thinning with enough water to give 500 ml (scant pint; 2¼ cups) if using thick cream. Add the sugar lumps, and heat to dissolve them. Lightly whisk the egg yolks to mix thoroughly, then slowly pour on the boiling cream, stirring all the time. Strain back into the pan through a fine-meshed sieve, and heat to thicken over a moderate heat, stirring continuously, until the custard will coat the wooden spoon. Using ingredients in these proportions, you should have a very smooth sauce. Allow to cool.

Purée the raspberries in the liquidizer with 3 leaves of mint, then strain through a fine sieve and reserve in a cool place. Add to the cold custard, a tablespoonful at a time; the intention is to flavour rather than colour it. Keep cold.

To serve, place a peach in each dish, and fix a small bunch of mint in the top of the fruit. Although the peaches should be at room temperature, surround with a few spoonfuls of the custard, well chilled, handing the rest round in a jug. To eat the sweet without difficulty dessert spoons and forks are necessary.

Cream caramel

This is one of the simplest sweets, but the cooking operation requires care. The cream is placed in a bain-marie containing a depth of 5 cm (2 in) water, which must never boil, and its surface should hardly colour. In this way, the cream becomes fine and smooth, without any holes.

For 6, to	310 g (10¾ oz; 1½ cups) sugar
fill a	1 litre (1¾ pints; 4½ cups) milk
charlotte	1 vanilla pod, or 2 teaspoons (1 sachet) vanilla
mould of	sugar
1 litre	a pinch of salt
(1¾ pints;	9 eggs
4½ cups)	
capacity	

Begin by making the caramel. Have ready a glass containing 2 tablespoons cold water, to halt the cooking of the sugar when it has reached the right colour, and have the mould to hand. Put 150 g (5¼ oz; ¾ cup) of the sugar into a saucepan, moisten with a little water, not too much, and cook over a moderate heat. When it starts to colour a light golden, watch it all the time and, as soon as it deepens to a dark brown, stop the cooking by pouring on the cold water—off the fire and with care, as it will splutter. When it has ceased bubbling, pour immediately into the mould, without attempting to smear it around. Leave to cool; it will set to a very thick syrup.

Preheat the oven to 200°C/400°F/Mark 6. Boil the milk, with the vanilla pod (if used) split lengthwise. Off the heat, add the rest of the sugar, the vanilla sugar if necessary, and the salt. Separate 5 of the eggs, and beat the yolks with the 4 whole eggs in a bowl. Pour on the milk, whisking all the time, then strain through a fine sieve, to catch the skin of the milk and traces of egg, onto the set caramel in the mould. Place in a bain-marie filled with cold water, and put in the oven. After 25–30 minutes, lower the temperature to 180°C/350°F/Mark 4, and keep an eye on the water to make sure that it does not boil. After 1 hour of cooking, test to see if the cream is done by inserting the blade of a knife into the middle; it should come out clean. Open the oven door and, 10 minutes later, take out the mould.

Allow to cool, then cover with a sheet of foil and refrigerate for 24 hours. To unmould, run the blade of a knife all round the edge of the mould, and turn out onto a dish with the caramel on top. The sweet is most delicate if left for at least 24 hours after cooking and served very cold.

Caramel mousse

This is composed of egg whites, whisked very stiff and cooked by the heat of the caramel, which is poured on in a thin stream, like oil for a mayonnaise, while continuing to whisk. It is served very cold, but not frozen, with a light egg custard.

For 6, to	butter
fill a	5 eggs
charlotte	360 g (12½ oz; 1¾ cups) sugar
mould of	2 sachets of vanilla sugar (about 2 teaspoons)
1 litre	
(1¾ pints;	
4½ cups)	
capacity	

Butter the mould, and reserve in a cool place. Separate the eggs (reserving the yolks for the custard), and whisk the whites to a firm snow. Then gradually incorporate 200 g (7 oz; 1 cup) of the sugar and the vanilla sugar, and continue whisking until the whites have developed a pearly gloss and have the consistency of shaving foam.

Then make the caramel. Wet the rest of the sugar in a saucepan with just enough water to moisten, not too much. Cook over a moderate heat and, when it has reached a pale golden colour, watch very carefully as the caramel will continue to cook with its own heat. At the end, it should be a deep brown, almost mahogany, and smell very strong. Pour the piping hot caramel onto the egg whites in a thin stream, whisking all the time, and go on whisking for a few minutes to spread the heat through the mixture. Turn into the mould, and allow to cool.

When the mousse is cold, cover it with a sheet of foil, and put in the refrigerator (not the freezer) overnight, or for at least 4 hours. When the time comes to serve it, soak the mould in water at room temperature or just slightly warmed, and turn out the mousse onto a serving dish. Surround with custard, made with the egg yolks and 500 ml (scant pint; 2½ cups) milk, sweetened and flavoured with vanilla.

Orange marmalade

This is made in February, when Seville oranges are available. They are steeped in water for 24 hours, twice, and then weighed in order to calculate the amount of sugar required.

For 1 kg	6–7 Seville oranges
(2 lb 4 oz)	1 lemon
marmalade	sugar, according to the weight of the fruit

If you are certain that the skin of the citrus fruits has not been treated with chemicals, simply wash them in cold water; but, if in any doubt, brush them in warm soapy water and rinse. With a very sharp knife on a board, slice the whole fruit into extremely thin rounds. Reserve the pips, and put them in a muslin bag. Weigh the fruit, and then transfer to a bowl, pour in 1 litre (1¾ pints; 4½ cups) cold water for every 500 g (1 lb 2 oz), and leave to macerate for 24 hours.

Turn into a preserving pan, bring to the boil, and cook for 15–20 minutes. Then return to the bowl, and steep for another 24 hours.

Weigh the fruit just before cooking, and put into the pan, together with the water and pips, adding 600 g (1 lb 5 oz; 3 cups) sugar per 500 g (1 lb 2 oz) of fruit. Cook over a moderate heat for about 1 hour, until the peel is transparent. Allow to cool a little before pouring into jars, so that the fruit does not rise to the top.

Pumpkin jam

You will be surprised by the beautiful golden colour and delicacy of this jam, the last of the winter.

> 3 kg (6 lb 12 oz) prepared pumpkin
> 3 kg (6 lb 12 oz; 15 cups) sugar
> 3 oranges
> 3 lemons

Remove the seeds and skin from the pumpkin, and cut the flesh into cubes of 3–4 cm (1½ in). Put the sugar into a preserving pan, just moisten with water, and cook over a moderate heat until it reaches the stage where a thread can be lifted with a skimmer and will shatter like glass (hard crack degree). Then add the pumpkin, the peel of the lemons, and the lemon and orange juice. Cook until the pumpkin is almost softened, stirring occasionally.

Then strain the liquid into another pan, and cook until you have a thick syrup which will coat the skimmer. Return the pumpkin to the pan, and boil for 5 minutes, stirring without crushing the fruit. Take off the heat, allow to cool slightly, and pour into jars, which you have previously filled with boiling water and drained. Seal the jars the next day, and eat after a week.

Rhubarb jam

This jam has the best flavour when made with mature spring rhubarb, towards the end of May.

> 3 kg (6 lb 12 oz) rhubarb
> 3 kg (6 lb 12 oz; 15 cups) granulated sugar
> a nut of butter

Wash the rhubarb and wipe dry. In the spring you can often leave the flat part of the sticks unpeeled, but test to see if they are too tough, and remove if necessary. Cut into chunks 1 cm (½ in) long, weigh, and put into a bowl with the same weight of sugar. Mix and leave to macerate overnight.

The next morning turn the contents of the bowl into a sieve or colander, set over a preserving pan to collect the juice. Cook over a moderate heat until reduced by half, then add the rhubarb and turn up the heat, stirring from time to time. When there is plenty of scum on the surface, put the nut of butter in the middle, which will drive the scum to the edges. Skim, lower the heat, and simmer until the jam will coat the back of the skimmer. Stir often at the end, for this jam, as it thickens, burns and sticks easily. Pour into jars and seal immediately. Wait 24 hours before tasting.

American cheesecake

The secret of success here is to use cream cheese which has been well drained. It rises during cooking, sometimes in a most disorderly way, but don't be put off: once the cake is cooked, you can fashion any uneven bits to fit the mould and, since it has to cool a little before turning out onto a rack, it will end up a good shape.

For a cake	500 g (1 lb 2 oz) well-drained cream cheese
mould of	100 g (3½ oz; ¾ cup) flour
25 cm (10 in)	4 eggs
diameter and	200 g (7 oz; 1 cup) caster sugar
6 cm (2½ in)	300–500 ml (½ pint-scant pint; 1¼–2¼ cups) milk
depth	1 orange or lemon
	5 digestive biscuits (crackers)
	250 g (8¾ oz) raspberry jam
	butter

Sift the flour, separate the eggs, and grate the peel of the orange or lemon. Butter the mould, and line the bottom with the crumbled crackers. Cover with a layer of the jam, spooning it in carefully without dislodging the crumbs stuck to the butter.

Preheat the oven to 200°C/400°F/Mark 6. Mix the cheese with the flour, egg yolks and half the sugar in a bowl. Gradually incorporate the milk, adding as much as the mixture will absorb. The resulting paste should be like a very smooth gruel, slightly heavy and falling from the spoon in unbroken folds. Flavour with the orange or lemon peel. Whisk the egg whites very firm, and fold in with the rest of the sugar, lifting the mass without stirring or beating. Pour into the mould to come up to 1.5 cm (½ in) of the top, and bake in the oven for 30 minutes. Then lower the heat to 150°C/300°F/Mark 2, and cook for a further 1 hour, keeping an eye on the colour. This delicious cake will keep in a cool place for more than a week.

Cherry cake

A homely but most delicious cake, which will keep fresh for several
days.

For a cake   500 g (1 lb 2 oz) ripe black cherries
tin of 24 cm   150 g (5¼ oz; ⅝ cups) thick cream
(10 in)   150 g (5½ oz; ¾ cup) sugar
diameter   275 g (9½ oz; 1⅞ cups) flour
                  1 sachet or 1 heaped teaspoon dried yeast
                  5 eggs
                  4 tablespoons Kirsch (optional)
                  150 ml (¼ pint; ⅝ cup) milk
                  20 g (¾ oz; ⅛ cup) butter
                  extra sugar

Wash, destalk and stone the cherries, and reserve. Mix the cream
and sugar in a bowl, stirring until the sugar is almost dissolved. Sift
the flour into a separate bowl, with the yeast. Add 3 yolks of egg and
2 whole ones, and mix, at the same time gradually incorporating the
sweetened cream and the Kirsch. Work the mixture until it is smooth
and without lumps, but remaining very heavy. Soften it by adding the
milk, but pouring in only one third at a time, since types of flour vary
in their powers of absorption, and the batter must be heavy enough to
support the cherries.

Preheat the oven to 200°C/400°F/Mark 6. Butter the cake tin and
sprinkle with sugar. Whisk the 3 egg whites to a firm snow, and fold
them into the mixture with the usual precautions, lifting the mass
without stirring or beating. Pour two-thirds into the tin, scatter the
cherries on top, and cover with the remaining one third. The tin
should be filled to within 1 cm (⅜ in) of the top. Put in the oven,
positioned on the middle rung, and bake for 45 minutes. Then test to
see if it is done by inserting the blade of a knife into the middle; it
should come out clean, with no liquid mixture clinging. Take the cake
out of the oven, allow to cool slightly, and then turn out onto a rack to
cool completely.

Lyonnais cake

Pink sugared almonds and fruit, fresh or in syrup, in a light base—this cake is easy to make, and is often served with a bowl of fresh cream.

For a cake	200 g (7 oz; ⅞ cup) butter
tin of	200 g (7 oz; ¾ cup) caster sugar
24 cm (10 in)	4 eggs
diameter	200 g (7 oz; 1⅜ cup) flour
	1 teaspoon vanilla sugar
	1 teaspoon dried yeast
	2 ripe pears, or in syrup
	500 g (1 lb 2 oz) ripe apricots, or in syrup
	12 pink sugared almonds
	extra butter
	icing sugar

If you are using fruit in syrup, drain carefully. Cut the pears into thin slices, and halve and stone the apricots. Crush the sugared almonds roughly. Butter the cake tin.

Preheat the oven to 180°C/350°F/Mark 4. To make the cake, whisk the softened butter and sugar together and, when they are well integrated, add the eggs one by one, mixing in thoroughly each time. When the mixture is frothy, incorporate the sifted flour, together with the vanilla sugar and yeast. Pour the mixture into the tin to a depth of 1.5 cm (½ in), and arrange the pears over the top. Cover with another thin layer of cake mixture, followed by the apricot halves with the hollow side down, then the almonds, and finally top with the rest of the cake mixture.

Put in the oven and, after 10 minutes, lower the heat to 160°C/315°F/Mark 2–3 for the next 15 minutes, and then again to 140°C/275°F/Mark 1 for the last 30 minutes. Turn off the oven, but leave the cake inside for another 10 minutes; altogether, it will have had 65 minutes of cooking. Allow to cool, turn onto a rack, and serve sprinkled with icing sugar.

Choux pastry

In its sweet version, this is the pastry of cream choux puffs and éclairs, pastry rings and, fried, the airy fritters known as 'pets de nonnes' of the Shrovetide Carnival. In savoury form, choux pastry is used for Dauphine potatoes and gougère—the Burgundy cheese cake (see p. 103). It is easy to make, but hard work when you add the eggs. If you want to make choux pastry in large quantities, don't increase the proportions of the ingredients, but use the basic amounts and repeat for several batches. Choux pastry wrapped in foil will keep for several days in the refrigerator.

For 12–15   75 g (2½ oz; ⅓ cup) butter
choux puffs   1 tablespoon sugar (for sweet pastry)
                 150 g (5½ oz; 1 cup) flour
                 4–5 eggs, and 1 extra for glazing

Pour 250 ml (scant ½ pint; 1⅛ cups) water into a large saucepan, and bring to the boil with the butter, salt and sugar. Add the flour all at once, stirring with a wooden spatula, and cook until the mixture comes away from the sides of the saucepan. Turn off the heat, and work for another minute. Add the first egg, whole, and work energetically until it is completely incorporated; all the elasticity of the pastry hinges on this first egg. Add the 3 other eggs one at a time, mixing in thoroughly each time, and then work the dough for at least another minute to firm it.

The usual number of eggs for the proportions given here is four, but not all pastry reacts in the same way. This one should be heavy without being hard, and compact. If it does not fit this description you will have to use a fifth egg, not whole but beaten, adding it by means of a tablespoon and incorporating it with the same care as the others. At the correct consistency, the dough should not collapse on the baking sheet, but keep its given shape.

Preheat the oven to 200°C/400°F/Mark 6, 15 minutes in advance, and grease a baking sheet. Pipe out the pastry from a forcing bag, fitted with a number 12 nozzle, into little heaps the size of an egg, evenly spaced on the baking sheet. Glaze each one with the beaten egg, using a pastry brush. Put in the oven, on the middle rung, and bake for 20–25 minutes; do not open the door before 20 minutes. When they are cooked, leave the puffs in the oven for 5 minutes with the door open, to firm.

Shortcrust pastry

This is the most quickly made and most useful of pastries, equally good for savoury preparations such as quiches, and sweet flans or fruit tarts.

For a tart	200 g (7 oz; 1⅜ cups) flour
tin of	a pinch of salt
24–26 cm	1 teaspoon sugar (for sweet pastry)
(10 in)	1 yolk of egg (optional)
diameter	100 g (13½ oz; ½ cup) butter
	extra butter and flour

Sift the flour onto the worktop or board, and make a well in the centre. Put into the middle the salt, sugar and egg yolk if used, the slightly softened butter and half of glass of very cold water. Knead together with the tips of your fingers, without working the dough, so that the flour is rapidly absorbed. Since types of flour vary in their powers of absorption, add the rest of the water by degrees, to obtain a paste which is supple without being soft, and is grainy and only just integrated. Above all, do not attempt to make a smooth dough at this stage; it would be like cardboard after cooking. Stop kneading as soon as all the flour is amalgamated, roll into a ball, and wrap in foil. Leave to rest in a cool place for at least 30 minutes, even up to 8 hours if you want to keep it for the next day.

   Preheat the oven to 230°C/450°F/Mark 8. Grease the tart tin with butter, using a pastry brush, sprinkle with flour, and turn upside down to get rid of the excess. Flour the worktop, and roll out the pastry twice, without kneading, folding it in half each time. It should be smooth and supple but, if not, roll it out a third time. Finally, roll it out to a thickness of 4 mm (¼ in), wrap round the rolling pin and transfer to the tart tin. Do not stretch the pastry at the edges as you line the tin, but rather make it flexible to allow for shrinkage by the heat. Wet your fingers and pinch up a ridge around the edge, then trim away the surplus pastry. Prick the base with a fork to prevent it rising, even if it will contain a heavy or creamy filling. If baking blind, cut out a round of greaseproof paper larger than the bottom of the tin, make perpendicular cuts all round the edge with scissors so that it will come to the top of the tin, and fit into the pastry. Sprinkle with fruit kernels or dried beans, more thickly at the edges, and prick the base through the paper.

Put in the oven, positioning on the lowest rung—pastry bases are often spoilt by lack of cooking. Bake until the edges are stiff. If you are adding a creamy filling, remove the paper, fill and return to the oven for about 5–10 minutes, keeping an eye on the colour.

Sweet flan pastry

This pastry is suitable for tarts where the filling is not cooked, or only briefly, for instance fresh strawberries or raspberries, stewed fruit or fruit in syrup, and creamy preparations.

For a tart 125 g (4¼ oz; ½ cup) butter
tin of 75 g (2½ oz; ⅜ cup) caster sugar
24–26 cm a pinch of salt
(10 in) 1 egg
diameter 250 g (8¾ oz; 1⅝ cups) flour
extra butter and flour

Work the butter, sugar and salt to a paste in a bowl. Add the whole egg, and incorporate so that the mixture is smooth and amalgamated. Sift the flour, and add all at once, mixing by hand. Then turn onto the worktop and knead, using the palm of your hand rather than the fingertips, until all the flour is absorbed. When it is smooth, roll into a ball, and cut into 4 with a knife. Pile the quarters of dough on top of each other, pressing with your hands or beating with a rolling pin. Repeat twice more, and leave to rest in a cool place for 1 hour.

Preheat the oven to 200°C/400°F/Mark 6. Butter and very lightly flour the tart tin. Roll out the pastry to a thickness of 5 mm (¼ in), then roll loosely round the rolling pin, transfer to the tin and line it. Cut out a round of foil larger than the tin, and make perpendicular cuts with scissors all round the edge so that it fits comfortably round the sides of the pastry and holds them up. Fill with dried beans or fruit kernels, and prick the base through the foil with the point of a knife. Put in the oven, bake for 15 minutes and then check; the sides of the pastry should be firm, with no risk of them collapsing. Remove the foil and beans, and return to the oven to finish cooking. Do not allow the pastry to brown, and keep an eye on the base which should become stiff. The pastry is now ready for use during the next day or two.

Pastry puffs with Roquefort cheese

These little patties can be served as cocktail snacks, or as a light, hot entrée, depending on their sizes. The recipe uses frozen puff pastry, and from one packet of pastry you can make 14–16 miniature patties, shaping them with a pastry cutter of 4.5 cm (2 in) diameter.

For 6–8   2×250 g (8 oz) packets of frozen puff pastry
300 g (10½ oz) Roquefort cheese
flour
butter
1 egg yolk

Thaw the frozen pastry in the bottom of the refrigerator for about 12 hours; it should become workable but remain cold. Keep the cheese at room temperature.

Lightly flour the worktop or board, and roll out the pastry to a thickness of 4–5 mm (¼ in), keeping it an even shape as far as possible. Cut out an even number of rounds, using a pastry cutter or thin glass of 4.5–5 cm (2 in) diameter. Lightly butter and flour a cold baking sheet, and place half the pastry rounds on this as they are ready. Put the equivalent of a large nut of cheese in the middle of each, carefully moisten the pastry around the cheese with a small pastry brush, without damping the edges of the round, and cover with a pastry round from the worktop, pressing with your fingers to make it stick.

Heap the rest of the pastry together without kneading, which would knock the air out. Roll out as before, and repeat the previous operation until all the pastry is used up. Heat the oven to the maximum temperature, and meanwhile glaze the patties with the egg yolk, thinned with 1 teaspoon water, painting each one twice. Make sure that the glaze does not collect round the edges, which would prevent the pastry rising. Place the baking sheet on the lowest rung of the oven; the pastry will quickly triple in volume, but don't open the door before 10–12 minutes. The cooking generally takes 15 minutes.

Then turn off the oven, half open the door and wait for 5 minutes to allow the pastry to firm. The patties will not sink when you take them out.

Cinnamon apple pie

All pastries involving apples are well received at the end of a meal. If apple tart is easy to make, apple pie is even simpler. Try it.

For a tart tin of 26 cm (10 in) diameter	1×500 g (1 lb) packet of frozen puff pastry butter, flour 5 apples 4 tablespoons sugar ½ teaspoon powdered cinnamon 1 egg

If possible choose frozen puff pastry in a roll, which is easier to use for this pie. But whatever type you have, it must thaw out thoroughly, allowing 12 hours in the bottom of the refrigerator.

Roll out the pastry to a thickness of 4 mm (¼ in), and divide into two, one part larger than the other. Lightly butter and flour the tart tin, and line the base with the smaller round of pastry, reserving the other for the lid. Allow the pastry to come over the edge of the tin, and prick the bottom with a fork. Peel and core the apples, cut into small dice and arrange in the pastry base, filling it right to the edge. Mix the sugar and cinnamon together, and sprinkle over the apples.

Preheat the oven to 220°C/425°F/Mark 7, 20 minutes in advance. Separate the egg and, with a pastry brush, paint the white all round the overlapping edge of the pastry base. Roll out the other round of pastry, wrap it round the rolling pin and lift onto the tart. Press the edges of the lid and base together to seal, and trim away all the surplus pastry. With the point of a knife, trace out diamond shapes on the lid, and glaze with the egg yolk mixed with a little water.

Put in the oven on the lowest rung and, after 15 minutes, lower the heat to 180°C/350°F/Mark 4. Then bake for 40–45 minutes, keeping an eye on the colour. Serve warm with, if desired, a bowl of plain fresh cream.

Lemon tart

This is made with a base of sweet flan pastry (see p. 237). If prepared well it is always a success, and can be a fitting end to a very elegant dinner.

For a tart	2 lemons
tin of	3 eggs
24–26 cm	150 g (5¼ oz; ¾ cup) sugar
(10 in)	100 g (3½ oz; ¾ cup) ground almonds (optional)
diameter	150 g (5½ oz; ⅝ cup) butter
	1 pastry base of partly cooked sweet flan pastry (see p. 237)

THE MERINGUE (optional)
2 whites of egg
a pinch of salt
100 g (3½ oz; ½ cup) caster sugar
icing sugar

If the lemons have been treated and protected by a skin of paraffin, wash and brush them in warm water. Grate the peel, and squeeze the juice. Whisk the eggs together with the sugar, the grated lemon peel, the juice of 1 lemon, and the ground almonds (if used). When the sugar has dissolved in the mixture, add the warm melted butter. Taste; the lemon flavour should be neither sharp nor mild, so if you need to add more lemon juice, do so by the teaspoonful.

Preheat the oven to 180°C/350°F/Mark 4. Fill the pastry base with the mixture; it should be half cooked, with the sides firm enough so that they do not collapse. Bake in the oven for 30 minutes, keeping an eye on the colour and the progress of the cooking.

If you want to make lemon meringue tart, proceed as above. Then whisk the egg whites very stiffly, together with the salt, and, from the moment they start to turn from a froth to a firm snow, incorporate the sugar in small amounts. Pipe the meringue out of a forcing bag, fitted with a number 10 nozzle, to cover the surface of the tart, beginning at the edge and working into the middle. Sprinkle with icing sugar, and colour in a slow oven (100°C/210°F/Mark ¼ or less). Watch it and, if necessary, leave the oven door half open.

Prûne tart

This is made with a base of sweet flan pastry, which is placed directly on a baking sheet. It is a large tart, and one for a special occasion. If possible use Agen prunes and ones that are vacuum-packed, which makes them less dry.

For a tart	500 g (1 lb 2 oz) prunes
of 30 cm	250 g (8¾ oz; 1 cup) butter
(12 in)	150 g (5¼ oz; ¾ cup) sugar
diameter	a pinch of salt
	2 eggs, and 1 extra for glazing
	500 g (1 lb 2 oz; 3⅜ cups) flour
	raspberry jam or redcurrant jelly

Stone the prunes by opening lengthwise with a small pointed knife, close them up again, and leave to soak for 3 hours in warm water. Then drain and wipe dry; they should have swelled up without disintegrating.

Make up the pastry, following the recipe for sweet flan pastry (p. 237). Lightly butter and flour the baking sheet. As soon as you have kneaded the dough, roll it out to a thickness of 4 mm (¼ in), and place on the baking sheet. Using a round dish as guide, trim round into a circle. Pinch up the edges; they need be no more than 1.5 cm (½ in) high, as there is no liquid in the filling. Reserve in a cool place for 30 minutes, together with the surplus trimmings of pastry.

Preheat the oven to 200°C/400°F/Mark 6. Fill the pastry case with the prunes. Roll out the pastry trimmings very thinly, cut into strips with a pastry wheel, and decorate the surface of the tart to give a lattice effect. Moisten the edges with water, and stick together without crushing. Glaze with the egg yolk, thinned with 1 teaspoon water. Place in the centre of the oven, and bake, keeping an eye on the colour. Test to see if the pastry is cooked by carefully lifting the edge of the tart; the base should be rigid. If it is too soft you will have to return it to the oven on a lower rung. Once cooked, allow the tart to cool, and fill the gaps in the surface with the jam.

Redcurrant and meringue tart

The cooked pastry base is filled with redcurrants in meringue, and finished in a slow oven for 1 hour without colouring.

For a tart
tin of 24 cm
(10 in)
diameter

THE FILLING
300 g (10½ oz) very ripe redcurrants
6 whites of egg
300 g (10½ oz; 1½ cups) caster sugar
100 g (3½ oz) hazelnuts
icing sugar

Make up the pastry, following the recipe for shortcrust (p. 236). Fit into the tart tin, and reserve in a cool place so that the pastry does not shrink during cooking.

Preheat the oven to 200°C/400°F/Mark 6. Line the pastry base with a sheet of greaseproof paper, prick the bottom with a fork through the paper, and sprinkle with dried beans. Put into the oven and bake until the sides are firm. Then remove the paper and beans, and finish cooking until the base is firm, without letting the pastry colour. Take out, and allow the oven to cool down.

Remove the stalks from the redcurrants. Lightly grill the hazelnuts, and crush them. Whisk the egg whites to stiff peaks, gradually incorporating the sugar as soon as they become frothy. Set aside 4-5 generous tablespoons of the mixture, and mix the redcurrants into the rest. Scatter the hazelnuts over the base of the cooked pastry case, spoon over the redcurrant meringue, and cover with the reserved egg whites. Smooth with a spatula, and sprinkle liberally with icing sugar. Put in the oven at 100°C/210°F/Mark ¼ or less, and bake without colouring for 1 hour. Serve warm or cold.

Tarte Tatin

This is an upside-down apple tart which made the reputation of two sisters who kept an inn at La Motte-Beuvron in the Sologne, near Orléans. It continued to be called 'la tarte des demoiselles Tatin', and even had its own special Tatin mould—a round tin 4–5 cm (2 in) deep. An ordinary cake tin has since replaced this.

For a tin of 24–26 cm (10 in) diameter	SWEET FLAN PASTRY 100 g (3½ oz; ⅜ cup) butter 100 g (3½ oz; ½ cup) sugar a pinch of salt 1 egg 250 g (8¾ oz; 1⅝ cups) flour

FILLING
2 kg (4 lb 8 oz) apples (preferably Cox)
200 g (7 oz; ⅞ cup) butter
200 g (7 oz; 1 cup) sugar
1 sachet of vanilla sugar, or a small pinch of cinnamon

Make up the pastry, following the recipe for sweet flan pastry (p. 237), and leave to rest in a cool place for 30 minutes.

Peel and core the apples, and cut into quarters. Melt the butter in the tin and, when it begins to foam, sprinkle in two thirds of the sugar, together with the vanilla sugar or cinnamon. Add the apples, arranging them in concentric circles, and cook over a moderate heat, without stirring but watching carefully, until the sugar has caramelized to a dark brown, running between the apple quarters.

Preheat the oven to 230°C/450°F/Mark 8. Roll out the pastry to a thickness of 4 mm (¼ in), and place on top of the tin, trimming off the edges by passing the rolling pin over it. Let the pastry fall in, but without trying to fit the edges into the tin, and prick in a few places with the point of a knife to prevent it rising.

Put in the oven, and bake until the pastry is golden and firm to the touch. Then cover with a sheet of greaseproof paper, lower the temperature to 180°C/350°F/Mark 4, and cook for another 10 minutes. Damp a cloth, and fold it in four. Take the tin out of the oven, place it on the cloth and leave for 10 minutes. Then put over a brisk heat for 1 minute, and turn the tart out of the tin, with the caramelized apples still in place. Serve warm with a jug of plain fresh cream.

Index

Barbara Griggs
The Home Herbal £1.95 .

As more and more people turn to alternative medicines and therapies, here is an authoritative and practical guide to herbal remedies, what they are, where to get them and how to use them. The book is organized alphabetically under the medical problems – for which conventional medicine can often fail or produce unpleasant side-effects, or in those minor cases where natural, gentle treatment is preferable – and herbal remedies are suggested under each of these headings – from acne to whooping cough. Additional chapters describe the preparation of herbal medicines, where to find herbs, and common and botanical names.

Claire Loewenfeld and Philippa Back
Herbs for Health and Cookery £2.50

'Not just a cookery book but a fascinating compendium on herbs; as cures for a host of ailments, as refreshing drinks both alcoholic and ''soft'', as beauty aids, as used in diets and invalid cooking and as a sheer delight to have around the house' SCOTSMAN

Roger Phillips
Wild Food £5.95

Companion to *Wild Flowers* and its bestselling sequels, here is a unique photographic guide to finding, cooking and eating wild plants, mushrooms and seaweed. From the multitude of safely edible species, Roger Phillips has selected the most attractive and appetizing. Alongside his beautiful photography, well-known wine and food writers such as Jane Grigson and Katie Stewart have contributed recipes.

Gail Duff
Gail Duff's Vegetarian Cookbook £2.95

Vegetarian eating is economical as well as nutricious. Beans, pastas, rice, eggs, cheese, vegetable curries, salads and more allow plenty of scope for the most mouthwatering menus.

'Develops meatless eating into authentic cuisine' THE TIMES

'Really imaginative . . . recipes anyone would be tempted to eat, vegetarian or not!' STANDARD

Katie Stewart
The Times Calendar Cookbook £2.95

A superb yearbook for the kitchen, containing a wide variety of recipes from winter soups, stews and casseroles to summer salads and picnic spreads. A complete guide to the most delicious and practical use of fruits, vegetables, fish, meat and game in season through the year.

'A truly superb cookery book' LEICESTER GRAPHIC

'A mouthwatering collection of recipes' HOUSE & GARDEN

Rita G. Springer
Caribbean Cookbook £1.75

Rita Springer, a leading expert on every aspect of Caribbean food, presents a whole spectrum of recipes, reflecting the influence of European, American and Chinese food as well as the traditional recipes of the islands. Includes a chapter on Caribbean kitchen equipment, a helpful glossary, and details of how to obtain the more unusual ingredients from British suppliers.

'Exciting cooking' SUN

Cook books

☐ **The Infra-Red Cook Book**	Kathy Barnes	£1.50p
☐ **The Microwave Cook Book**	Carol Bowen	£1.95p
☐ **Pressure Cooking Day by Day**	Kathleen Broughton	£2.50p
☐ **Cooking on a Shoestring**	} Gail Duff	£1.95p
☐ **Vegetarian Cookbook**		£2.95p
☐ **Crockery Pot Cooking**	Theodora Fitzgibbon	£1.50p
☐ **The Book of Herbs**	Dorothy Hall	£1.95p
☐ **The Best of**	Rosemary Hume and	
Cordon Bleu	Muriel Downes	£1.95p
☐ **Diet for Life**	Mary Laver and	
	Margaret Smith	£1.95p
☐ **Quick and Easy Chinese**		
Cooking	Kenneth Lo	£1.95p
☐ **Herbs for Health**	Claire Loewenfeld	
and Cookery	and Philippa Back	£2.50p
☐ **The Preserving Book**	Caroline Mackinlay	£4.50p
☐ **The Book of Pies**	Elisabeth Orsini	£1.95p
☐ **Learning to Cook**	Marguerite Patten	£2.50p
☐ **Complete International**		
Jewish Cookbook	Evelyn Rose	£2.95p
☐ **Caribbean Cookbook**	Rita Springer	£1.95p
☐ **The Times Cookery Book**	} Katie Stewart	£3.50p
☐ **Shortcut Cookery**		£1.95p
☐ **Freezer Cookbook**	Marika Hanbury Tenison	£1.95p
☐ **The Pan Picnic Guide**	Karen Wallace	£1.95p
☐ **Mediterranean Cooking**	Paula Wolfert	£1.95p

All these books are available at your local bookshop or newsagent, or
can be ordered direct from the publisher. Indicate the number of copies
required and fill in the form below   10

....

Name_____
(Block letters please)

Address_____

_____

Send to CS Department, Pan Books Ltd, PO Box 40, Basingstoke, Hants
Please enclose remittance to the value of the cover price plus:
35p for the first book plus 15p per copy for each additional book ordered
to a maximum charge of £1.25 to cover postage and packing
Applicable only in the UK

While every effort is made to keep prices low, it is sometimes
necessary to increase prices at short notice. Pan Books reserve
the right to show on covers and charge new retail prices which
may differ from those advertised in the text or elsewhere